Dancing
WITH
DEPRESSION

heart to heart,

Sharon

Dancing

WITH

DEPRESSION

*A Spiritual Pathway for Recovery from
Darkness to Light*

SHARON HIGHBERGER

TATE PUBLISHING
AND ENTERPRISES, LLC

Scripture quotations marked "NIV" are taken from the *Holy Bible, New International Version®*, Copyright © 1973, 1978, 1984 by International Bible Society. Used by permission of Zondervan Publishing House. All rights reserved.

Scripture quotations marked "Msg" are taken from *The Message*, Copyright © 1993, 1994, 1995, 1996, 2000, 2001, 2002. Used by permission of NavPress Publishing Group. All rights reserved.

Scripture quotations marked "CEV" are from the *Holy Bible; Contemporary English Version,* Copyright © 1995, Barclay M. Newman, ed., American Bible Society. Used by permission. All rights reserved.

The opinions expressed by the author are not necessarily those of Tate Publishing, LLC.

Published by Tate Publishing & Enterprises, LLC
127 E. Trade Center Terrace | Mustang, Oklahoma 73064 USA
1.888.361.9473 | www.tatepublishing.com

Tate Publishing is committed to excellence in the publishing industry. The company reflects the philosophy established by the founders, based on Psalm 68:11,
"The Lord gave the word and great was the company of those who published it."

Book design copyright © 2012 by Tate Publishing, LLC. All rights reserved.
Cover design by Jan Sunday Quilaquil
Interior design by Joana Quilantang

Published in the United States of America

ISBN: 978-1-62295-304-2
1. Self-help / Depression / Grief
2. Religion / Christian Life / Spiritual Growth
12.11.05

To all who hope to hope,
to friends "Angel", Pat and Lee who gave me hope,
and to Jude, Janene and Eric
whose unconditional love pierced the darkest times.

> Blessed are those who listen to me, watching daily at my doors, waiting at my doorway. For those who find me find life and receive favor from the LORD.
>
> Proverbs 8:34-35 (NIV)

Acknowledgments

To the One who delivers us from all darkness and death to raise us to new life, all praise and thanksgiving.

First and foremost to my husband and friend, Jude Highberger, who's wisdom throughout the journey encouraged me to "stay with the process", my love and gratitude. To Sr. Marcia Ziska, who inspired the writing of this book through her insight that the story of spiritual recovery from depression was not just for me, but for others, may all blessing return to you tenfold. There are no words to adequately express my appreciation for the gift of those who loved me unconditionally in my life with depression, and then had the heart to read the story hidden deeply in my mind, heart, and soul: Janene Falley, Mary Wright, Rose Anne Hubbard, Joyce Minson, Michelle Turney, Laura Will, and Pat Samson. My heartfelt gratitude to Sr. Linda Roth, Sr. Mary Pat Johnson, Rev. Edith Funk, Mary L. Vorsten, Marilyn and Ted Rodgers, Dr. David Console, Father Tom Aduri and Father William Bruning. Your feedback helped me to believe with hope in a purpose for the book and the meaning for its journey. To Jennifer Halling who's skills and spirit provided a safe place to begin public expression of my battle between mind and soul, darkness and light, you were gift.

TABLE OF CONTENTS

INTRODUCTION

I am a simple woman who was born and raised in Kansas. I married and had two children, divorced, and remarried. Yet, through the suffering I experienced in life-long depression, I have come to know that of which the mystics write:

> *God is the greatest desire of your heart and soul,* and you can know God in you, and you can live in God's love—which will dispel all the darkness in your soul.

I have, by most accounts, lived a very quiet and normal life in the Midwestern United States. However, beneath my exterior appearance was another life that others could not see and that even I did not recognize.

I saw my life as it appeared externally. I was a person caught up in the busyness and demands of being a mother and spouse and then a student, when I went back to school after having been a "stay-at-home mom." However, in the midst of life's difficulties, I eventually found an interior life hidden within my exterior shell. My only connection to this other life was a growing awareness of an interior joyless existence. At times I knew happiness and had fun, of course, but when I was quiet, the interior emptiness demanded to be acknowledged. Since high school, I have been aware of a yearning that led me to feel that there must be something more than this. I could not possibly have recognized or consciously described this interior yearning that clouded the light of day and dimmed my happy moments.

Since I was a child this yearning has been accompanied by depression, and today I am not sure I can separate the two. Was I physically born with this yearning imbedded in my soul? I suspect so, because the mystics write of the yearning for God as an innate part of the human being, even though we generally have little or no consciousness of it.

It is this consciousness, this awakening, this coming to myself of which I write in this book. I feel compelled to write about it because my lack of consciousness created in me an expansive desert of deep suffering—a separateness—that I might have been able to avoid had I been told that it is possible to connect to God directly here and now.

How can it be that I never understood that God connected to *me*? In my denominational upbringing we read about the saints and the mystics who write of intimately knowing God's love, but I did not grasp that what these women and men experienced *is also within me.* My education in a parochial school led me to perceive that closeness with God was for holy people and saints. My sense of an imperfect self automatically excluded closeness with God. It was implied that we should observe and admire the spiritual experiences of the mystics and saints from a respectful distance. I did not grasp that the envied relationship with God is also innate in me and in every soul that breathes on this earth. I realize now there is no separation from God but for what one thinks.

Intimacy with God is not just for saints and mystics. Intimacy with the divine is for the little Kansas woman raising a couple of kids, divorcing, remarrying, and slogging her way through depression. It is for the administrator buried under responsibilities, and for the checker at the grocery store. It is for the roadside maintenance crew and the volunteer cleaning out cages at the humane shelter. It is for the teacher who faces twenty-odd students every day and the police officer who scuffles with belligerent, errant souls. It is for the priest behind the altar and the little lost soul, alone and distraught, sitting in a corner shadow without a friend in the world.

Each and every person has the necessary connection to the ultimate, innate interior desire that can reveal the true Presence of his or her own soul. Each and every person has access to actual knowledge of the creative beauty that manifested who they truly are. Each and every person can find all that he or she would hope for within his or her own being.

It is not to the select alone—to prophets and mystics—that truth is revealed. The saints and mystics are only one avenue through which the experience, the reality, and the truth that each of us bears is made known. The door to realizing the experience of God and the truth of our own being in God is open for everyone. No one is barred out.

When we become conscious of that truth, we can see that our life roles have nothing much to do with anything that will remain eternal. Our life roles express only what we are to be about here; they are not who we are in God.

And thus we turn to the internal search. What we seek will not be found outside our self.

Getting caught up in the expression of our external life gives us a sense of control. Life seems attainable for the will and working of the ego's need to manage. In our exterior life we focus on one another, on what is to be accomplished, and on what is attainable.

What is *not* attainable, however, is what we ultimately want to fulfill in our interior selves—and the reason it is not attainable is because it is already ours! After all, we cannot attain what we already have, because it is ours already for the having. *What we must do, then, is to become conscious of it, of its working in us as a presence, as the source from which the expression of our living and loving comes.*

Much of my life's wanderings—the bumping into trees in the dark and dim night—might have been shortened, if not illuminated, had I become conscious of the truth sooner. Be that as it may, experiencing life as I did adds authenticity to what was revealed to me and also allows me to clearly state that all I have learned cannot be told but must be revealed to each individual.

Each person, then, must proceed on his or her own journey. Ideally, our response to the conscious awareness that our own ultimate desire to know God would guard our impulses to gratify our cravings in less than satisfying methods. Without a conscious appreciation for the innate longing for God, we unconsciously strive to fulfill the craving with what is less than gratifying. We tend then toward satisfying our desires with shopping, food, work, relationships and anything that seeks inner satisfaction other than God. The truths of our attachments must be reckoned with until we are freed to fully live in love and new life. The revelation that our ultimate desire is to know God can come through the very act of living out the spiritual experience of disentanglement from what is not satisfying, or at best is only temporary satisfaction.

All persons must discover, within their own story life, how they are entangled and what their wilderness is like. All persons, upon living their own story and having had the truth of their life revealed, recognize and recount their own liberating moments of understanding. Ultimately their final jubilation, through finding this freeing process, will then declare with new truth: *I am beloved of God, as I am so created.*

This is the ultimate truth of who you are. Truth is found through disengaging from life's busyness, whether it be the little actions you are about or the great moments of success that are noticeable across the globe, because ultimately, none of these matters. What matters is the story of your own discovery of self that finally acclaims, with all joy, the ultimate peace of your existence experienced as being one with God. On finding that discovery, you realize that the *kingdom is here as the heaven you seek.* The kingdom is now and forever. God is within you. You can come to know who you truly are, that your "I am" is never separate from God and you discover your place of being is within divine love. Love desires to reveal itself. The experience of love reveals the innate value of your being. Do these words create a subtle, tearful, joyful desiring resonance within your soul? If so, you already know within yourself that it is true, for the reverberation of your heart's response tells you so.

Still, love's truth is meant to be found. We are called to be attentive to that which is being revealed. Set aside time to pay attention to this revealing. Let it awaken. It is in quietness that you will find opportunities for awareness and attain the glimpse of promise in the doorway. The revelation will happen in the process of slowing down and in your willingness to meet the unveiling. It is courageous to admit that what you believe of yourself seems incongruent with what is revealed to you by God's love and that you are unable to let the two meet. It is courageous to admit that the shadows of the heart exist. It is the hopeful and courageous soul that declares, "I will take the darkness to God, who sees it already, and my hope of God's unconditional love reveals my soul to myself. When I can meet myself with all honesty and face who I am while believing I am unconditionally loved, then and only then can my soul be satisfied."

When you are honest and satisfied and do not judge; when only understanding and compassion remain; and when, in your own mirror, you see the love of God looking into your own eyes, then you will see clearly what others have seen. You too will say, "I am awakened today. I have experienced that of which the mystics write and I, too, am at peace, for I have found the ultimate satisfaction of my soul. God is within me."

In the retelling of my story I became more aware of God's presence, particularly in significant times of difficulty or transition. New awakenings developed into reflection questions that are provided at the end of this book. It is my hope through personal reflection or group study you also find the Sacred Presence in your own story.

WHERE DOES
GRACE BEGIN?

The transformation that changed the *center* focus of my life began in the early 1980s, after my seemingly orderly existence was rocked by a significant marital crisis. The crisis triggered a deep depression. I was completely devastated and found myself praying for help. I was in such a depressed state that I was not even able to get out of bed in the morning to help my children get ready for school.

Crisis confronts the reality of our helpless vulnerability and how we see the world, creating spiritual questions: Where is God? Am I alone? Why did God let this happen to me? Why didn't God protect me? Crisis creates a loss of safety and security and shakes our ego's need for a firm, reliable foundation of a manageable, predictable life. In crisis, we describe ourselves as feeling torn apart. Our prayer becomes as primitive as an infant. Where are You? Help me.

Through meditation's quieting of the mind, I began to hear guidance: I was to do volunteer work at my church. In spite of this message, I resisted leaving the house and going out in public. I didn't believe I could function well enough to work. "How can I?" I argued with God. "Look at me! I can't even manage to get the kids ready for school, and you want me to go to work?"

And yet, eventually I was able to gather enough faith and courage to connect with the church as a place to volunteer. Volunteering occupied my thoughts, gave me the motivation to get up each day, and helped counteract my depression. I found that the volunteer work gave purpose and meaning to my personal life, and after a while it led to a paid secretarial position. As it turns out, the inner urge I had to volunteer was a sign that I was developing the resources within myself to nurture my own spirit. Volunteering and stepping out of my comfort zone represented the first time I consciously made myself available, attentive, and responsive to God's presence in my life.

After a few years, I became restless. My ability and skills had grown to the point that I was maxing out mentally and emotionally in my secretarial position. I was getting tired and had trouble keeping up with work's demands, and I was beginning to make mistakes. However, the thought of quitting my job was unsettling, because working for the church seemed like the *right* thing to do.

At the same time I had this restless urge to move forward in a different direction, I felt a contrasting pull to stillness, to quiet, to doing nothing. Finally, one Wednesday, I decided to go sit in the empty church during my lunch hour. My initial effort to sit quietly was significantly short in duration—after only about five minutes, I was out of there! I couldn't tolerate the silence or the inactivity. The desire was to sit quietly and to not think by just focusing on my breath. I would later discover this meditation practice is called "contemplation" or "centering prayer."

Nonetheless, I remained faithful to my Wednesday lunch dates with solitude. My ability to become quiet developed naturally, and my periods of sitting in silence gradually lengthened. Even though it seemed to go against the grain of my type A personality, and I was frustrated at times because I couldn't seem to quiet my mind, I stayed with the practice. Or perhaps I should say, the practice stayed with me.

One day I remember being particularly exasperated. My mind kept wandering in response to worries and my busy schedule, and I commented to God in a rather off-hand manner that I wasn't doing very well with quieting my mind. And then, something changed.

I sensed it first in my body, as I realized that I was physically relaxed—warm, even. I thought to myself, *What's happening? It almost feels like I'm being hugged!* I felt like I was in a gentle but firm embrace, as if God were saying, "It's okay. You're here." Oh, my—I had just been hugged by God!

Until then, before I had the physical experience of being hugged, I honestly thought I was just sitting quietly in church as a form of prayer. It never crossed my mind that in doing so I might experience God. In my quiet prayer at home I sometimes had a sense of presence, but this feeling of being hugged by God was a breakthrough to a new type of awareness; it increased my determination to be faithful to my weekly practice of sitting in stillness.

My practice was becoming something much deeper though I did not yet know the deep workings within myself; however, I *did* know the experience of feeling hugged. I knew that God knew I was there. It didn't matter that being quiet and still was a struggle. I didn't have to do it well. The only condition seemed to be that I came.

Months later I had an opportunity to attend a one-day workshop on centering prayer. Although I wasn't aware of its history, I was amazed to discover that I already knew the basics of how to practice the prayer of stillness and listening:

- Create a sacred place for prayer

- Physically relax as you focus on the breath

- Allow thoughts to move on without becoming attached to them or giving them attention

- Remain in the stillness, trusting in the grace of God to honor your practice

- Be faithful to the practice

- Let go of expectations or wanting anything

I can now state unequivocally that this practice of being quiet and the desire for stillness began to be—and has remained—the connection to my life as it unfolded. Having time alone to connect with God each and every day has become my lifeline. What began as a desire to be quiet is now life itself, like a spiritual umbilical cord. It became such an assured way for me to connect with God. Years later, when I lost my job, I remained calm and immediately turned to meditation. I knew stillness would take me to *where* I needed to go.

MEDITATION AND SPIRITUAL PRACTICES

Meditation. The word itself makes many people shudder. Years ago, given my personality, if someone had said to me, "You should meditate," I would have laughed. At that time I would have had the same response most people do, "I can't sit still," "My mind never quits," "I'm too energetic," and the classic "I don't have time!" The reasons not to meditate are innumerable, but that in itself is a sign that one would be encouraged toward meditation.

My own motivation to meditate came from a growing dissatisfaction with my life. I was restless and felt the urge to move forward and do something different, even as my mind was telling me why I shouldn't leave my church secretarial position. The consternation left me frustrated and practically immobilized.

In this state of confusion, what drew me to meditation? Restlessness and the need to do something different motivated me to respond to a quiet urging from within to seek stillness. Other than to the quiet, I didn't know where to go. I had no idea where this desire to be quiet originated. The only awareness I had was that something in my life needed to change.

I felt like I was serving God by working for the church, and this thought made it difficult for me to leave that position. It had not dawned on me that the desire to do life differently entailed more than finding a new job. I did not see at the time that wanting to move forward, yet moving toward stillness was the working of the Spirit within me. I eventually realized that to find new life I needed to move away from the way of *doing* life that accentuated activities and move toward stillness instead.

Everything my life seemed to be about—raising children, struggling with a difficult marriage, discerning what kind of work to do and where to do it—was what I knew as life itself. But these activities were *not* life itself. Intertwined in the energies and life demands was an unobtrusive but consistent urge to come to the quiet. It wasn't as if I heard a voice saying directly, "Come and sit in the quiet stillness of my presence and you will come to know life and know it abundantly." Of course I had heard that call in Scripture readings, but the words had never moved beyond the level of my mind. Now the call was working from within me. My heart desired stillness. My body was asking for relaxation and less stress. My mind was quieting and I was beginning to listen with my heart, now that I knew God was aware of me.

Stillness reveals God's subtle, constant, ever-drawing, ever-requesting, ever-persistent desiring of us. In the midst of the chronic busyness, activity, priorities, and demands of life, it is important to pay attention to any little promptings you might have to be quiet and still. Attending to these promptings is a way of acknowledging that God really does desire you. Consider your yearning for stillness to be God's way of guiding your life that is hidden in the stillness. In the quiet you will become connected to what your life is yearning to be. You may not know yet that the life you seek is so much more than what you think it will be, should be, or could be, but nonetheless, life change is working in you. This process of a spiritual life is like two lovers finding each other and connecting together that creates your life.

It is in the quiet, when our mind is still, that we begin to sense that life encompasses more than our mind's efforts to figure out life and its directions. Something new and unforeseen seems to suddenly emerge out of darkness—like a seed sprouting from the dark earth. One day in the stillness I had the very clear and unquestionable awareness that I was not living out the Gospel directive to feed the hungry, to give drink to the thirsty, to clothe the naked, and to visit the imprisoned. It was clear to me that I needed to do just that.

Shortly afterward, I had lunch with a priest for whom I had been doing some secretarial work. He was the director of a homeless shelter. I shared my restlessness with work and my awareness that I wasn't living the Gospel as I thought I should.

He said, "Quit your job and come and work at the shelter as a volunteer."

I replied in disbelief, "Quit a paying full-time job to volunteer?" As it turns out, that's exactly what he was saying, and that's exactly what I did.

Now that I more fully realize how absolutely out of character it was for me to quit a paying job to volunteer, I smile. Indeed, in the years to come, I would be faced with the destruction that workaholism would create in my mind and soul. At the time I made this particular decision, though, I wasn't aware of that aspect of myself; I simply was restless for action. I had responded faithfully to a desire for stillness, and my life, hidden in the silence, suddenly burst forward with a decision I would not have thought to choose for myself. It was at the shelter that I found the desire of my heart, which was unrecognized until it was revealed in the change. I found it difficult to leave my position at the church because I wanted to serve God. At the shelter I found my something more—a call to ministry.

Stillness and quietude have never failed to result in the creation of new life. In fact, they could even be considered a lifeline. From where does life come? It comes from within you. Be still and listen.

Living in Grace

Although the significant changes in direction I under-went when I first became rooted in stillness were unchar-acteristic, it never dawned on me that these transitions were rooted in grace. What were the origins of this graced life movement? What was the spark, the igniter of such change?

During childhood, I lived with a depression that developed as a result of unresolved grief. The grief event occurred in the third grade. As a brownie in the Girl Scout program, the troupe worked for months to prepare for the annual Father/Daughter Banquet, which was the biggest event of my young life. We made placemats and centerpieces, and planned skits for entertainment. On the evening of the banquet, I skipped downstairs in my freshly washed, newly pressed Brownie uniform, wearing all the badges I had earned on a sash.

As I entered the kitchen, my grandfather, Gramp, popped his head in the back door and asked, "Are you ready to go?"

Puzzled, I look at my mother and said, "I thought Daddy was going with me?"

Mother replied with irritation, "I told you, he has to work, but Gramp is going with you." And off we went. I'm sure Mother had told me earlier that Gramp would be taking me, but it just didn't register because in my young mind it was dads who went to Father/Daughter Banquets.

I can still see myself sitting at one of the white tables in the gymnasium. I looked around and thought, *I'm the only one here with her grandpa. Everyone else has their dad. I must not be as important as work.* A red ball of energy welled up inside me. My rage was the pain of Dad's choice to work. My child's mind perceived that I was not the value. As I turned to Gramp, I started to project this feeling onto him, but I remember thinking, *I can't be angry at Gramp; I love him,* and immediately the red energy rolled back into me. I believe this event was the root of my grief that developed into depression.

Throughout my childhood I thought work was more important than me. Dad worked two jobs; during the day he was creating and building a family business, and then he worked the second shift at the Goodyear tire plant. I have a photograph of my dad and me when I was about three years old, but otherwise I have no memory of us being alone together. I have wonderful memories of family occasions, but I needed a child's relationship with her father.

Also contributing to my frail emotional health was my perception mother was very overwhelmed, anxious, and unable to manage all of us kids. By eleven years old, I, too, was feeling the overwhelming responsibility of caring for six younger siblings. The focus on work that needed to be done in the home left the impression that I was not important, except to take care of my brothers and sisters. Underlying the banquet episode where I lost my father/daughter attachment was a lack of attachment to my mother due to the household demands.

Difficulties I experienced at school because of depression's perceived inadequacies added to my unhappiness. If it hadn't been for my relationship with my dear, dear grandmother, Nora, I would have been without a significant adult connection in my life. I was driven by the unquestioned belief that no one loved me and I was not worthy enough to deserve attention. No one recognized that I was in a significant depression.

I was about thirteen years old when I first attempted to kill myself. I planned to stand on the opposite corner from the bus stop, so the driver would not slow down to pick me up, and then throw myself in front of the bus when it passed. I had no thoughts of how others would be affected by my actions. I was intent on my plan. However, just as the bus approached and I was physically projecting myself toward it, a voice from within said with such force, "Go to church!" that it threw me back from my forward momentum, nearly knocking me off balance. With the summer dust swirling in the hot air, I watched with disappointment as the bus sailed past me.

I walked to church and sat there, crying. As I write this, I'm just now realizing that it wasn't only in the 1980s that I was drawn to a still church—it also happened in the 1960s, when I was in crisis as a child. I cried in the empty church for a long time. Eventually I went home, sat on my bed, and continued crying, repeating over and over, "No one loves me." Suddenly, a very clear, "God loves you" interrupted my ruminating mind.

Now, here was a new thought for a child raised in a parochial system: "God loves me." And then, a story formed in my mind as a single thought: A young girl walked to her farm pond every day, and every day a stranger met her there. They threw rocks in the pond, used sticks to poke at creatures, and talked and talked quite companionably. One day, starting up the road to her home, the girl turned to say something to the one who was a stranger, yet a friend. However, he was nowhere in sight! He had totally disappeared. The story concluded with the thought, "...and your friend will be with you every day of your life."

It wasn't until I was an adult that I realized my young life had been saved through actual divine intervention. Years later I finally understood that grace and compassionate love, connecting through story, initiated the healing power of writing for a little girl who only needed to know that God loved her and would be with her every day. When I was fourteen years old and in the eighth grade, I remember having such a strong desire for God that I wanted to go to a convent; however, I was told I was too young. I now believe these strong desire's for God, are really experiences of God's initiative of desiring and loving us. This desire for God, this yearning, expressed itself in what would become a life-long refrain: "There must be something more than this." Maybe it is the whisper of Spirit reminding us, "There is something more."

Another experience I recall vividly from that period was when a priest quizzed my parochial freshman high school class on the Baltimore Catechism. We answered his questions flawlessly by rote, but when he inquired as to the meaning of our responses, we were clueless! I remember the shock of realizing that I didn't know a thing about God.

Not until my high school senior retreat in 1966, given by a charismatic priest, would I find a sense of connecting with God. The priest wisely used the social justice act of demonstrations as a spiritual revival tool. We broke into small groups and made placards that promoted God and said, "Down with the devil." What a rally! No activity in the retreat had anything to do with learning *about* God or having the right answers. The entire retreat was relational. Our hearts found an enthusiasm for God, and we had a lively, fun-filled retreat (a first in my parochial upbringing!) involving the heart and soul, not the mind. We did not have to know anything, and I remember feeling relieved, peaceful, and connected again to my spirituality. The retreat experience of connecting with God through heart and soul felt like the *something more* for which I yearned.

I married in 1968 and moved out of state and away from my family and religious practices. I didn't decide to leave the church—I just didn't go until I had my second child, whom I wanted baptized. I also decided I needed to start attending church again for the sake of my children's formation.

In the late 1970s, my marriage was becoming increasingly difficult. I was taken by surprise when a friend said she thought my marital problems had to do with alcoholism. As it happened, my husband was from an alcoholic home, and I suspected alcoholism in my own family history. I went straight to Al-Anon, and I am indebted to this spiritual program for encouraging me to find a God of my own understanding. The Twelve Steps suggested I could find my own *relationship* with God. My religious upbringing left me focused more on being "good", than on a relationship.

Because of the difficulties in my marriage and my general state of unhappiness, I looked for help and made calls seeking support; but one appointment was cancelled and other persons I contacted didn't call back. Meanwhile, a cousin told me that we can come to God directly, just as we are. She also said we could live a life in God's Spirit *for the asking*.

Because no other avenues of help seemed to come forward, after communion one Sunday morning at mass, I prayed, "God, if you are there, you can have my life, and whatever this 'life in the Spirit' thing is, I want that, too."

Within a few months, my life was on a definite upward course. I was happier, I wasn't yelling at my children as much, and I was having a great time with new friends I found in Al-Anon. As I was growing in the awareness that I could invite God into my daily life, I distinctly remember standing in the center of my dining room, deciding who was going to be running the show—me or God. After some deliberation, I gave up control of my life, realizing I hadn't done such a good job thus far, considering my discordant marriage and general unhappiness. I was to discover how *surrender*—to let go to something greater than myself—was a powerful and wonderful experience of discovering how God relates to me and helps me in the unmanageable areas of my life.

One of those unmanageable areas was my inability to stop smoking. I had asked many people how to pray to stop smoking, as I had tried unsuccessfully seven times to quit on my own. My search for prayer was not satisfied until I found in a dusty bible the passage in Matthew 6 where we are told, if you don't know how to pray, say the Our Father. Saying this simple childhood prayer when I had the urge to smoke, I was able to cut back considerably to one cigarette a day. One day after twenty little girls in my daughter's Blue Bird Troup left the house, I turned to tobacco in the stress. That evening before going to bed I became quite impatient, reminding God I had asked for help in overcoming my addiction, but here I was smoking again! I reinforced that I *meant it* when I said I didn't want to smoke! I was heard!

I awakened sometime in the night; my body was rigid and sweating profusely. I heard a whishing sound. I saw a ghostlike leopard jump from the closet to my side three times, viciously clawing at my chest upon each return to me. I was terrified. Suddenly, the leopard was gone. My thought was that it was a nightmare, until I heard a voice say, "Do you dream in sound?" I admitted I did not, but then what was that? The next day I called a friend from church, thinking he would have some explanation, as he seemed to be in touch with a spirituality beyond our religious customs. He said I was probably delivered from a "spirit of nicotine," and he encouraged me to attend the Life In The Spirit Seminar. Within three months, not only was I totally free of the smoking addiction I had struggled with for more than ten years, I found the power of God intervening in my life. This surrender thing was a good deal! It worked great and all was well—but not for long.

One particular day, I vividly remember I had been reading about forgiveness. Now that God and I were communicating, I asked God if I would be forgiven if I did something terrible.

"Yes, you will be forgiven."

"Well, what if I….," naming another terrible thing.

"Yes, you will be forgiven."

And I named the worst offenses I could think of, "What if I committed adultery or murdered someone?'

"Yes, I would forgive you."

That very evening, when my husband was honest with me about something he had done that I previously would have considered unforgivable, I was, to some degree, spiritually prepared for what he had to say. However, the ensuing crisis in our marriage sent me into a major depression and to the floor of a dark closet, where I contemplated suicide. After considering methods I could use to kill myself, I heard an intervening thought: "You could try faith." Yes, I could try faith. My mental anguish ceased as if cut with a knife and I got up and walked out of the closet. Almost thirty years passed before I came to realize that the Spirit of Wisdom was with me in that closet and during that dark time of my life.

New desires occurred. While journaling had been a periodic practice before, it now became a daily practice and something new seemed to occur within the writing; I would journal until I was empty of all the pain and anguish, and then, after a period of quiet, a few words would come. If I wrote those words, the pen would flow. The words of faith, love, and encouragement that poured out of my pen saw me through my painful thoughts and feelings as I adjusted to my life crisis. The writings seemed to come from someplace other than myself, with wisdom beyond my knowledge or life experience.

It was difficult to face the reality of my thoughts and feelings within, but the encouragement to "come," "be still," and "know the source of your breath" kept me coming to the quiet, to stillness, to meditation, and to solace. Sitting in stillness, I believe, one begins to absorb the ways of something higher than one's self. I began to feel a sense of being encouraged.

Part of the encouragement I received was to return to college. At that time, the thought of continuing my education was terrifying, and I bawled my way up to the door of the administration office to enroll in college. Throughout my elementary school years in the 1950's, I sat at the dining room table many a night in tears as I tried to complete my homework. I knew the homework would be unsatisfactory and would result in a negative, embarrassing, and shaming event at school the next day. At the time children were mercilessly compared with each other, with the smart children being separated from the academically challenged or misbehaving.

I would not know until the 1990s that depression impairs the ability to focus, concentrate, and remember, to say nothing of the analytical abilities required for math. As a child, I thought all these difficulties in school meant there was something inferior about myself and my capabilities. I shudder today when I remember the trauma that my depression created during my childhood. I think of how many people suffer from this unrecognized illness and live alone with its consequences. So you can understand how terrified I was as an adult when I felt the desire to return to college. A hidden grace again was working in me, challenging me to discover whether the childhood belief in my lack of intelligence was, in fact, true.

Returning to college, leaving my job at the church office, and volunteering at the homeless shelter were big life steps. Another step developed when the shelter staff had the opportunity to participate in a career development program. To my great surprise, a hidden desire and call to ministry were revealed. *How can I be a minister?* I thought. I'm *a woman, I'm Catholic, I'm married, and I have children!* Despite all my inner protests, I entered a Clinical Pastoral Education program at the local Veterans Administration and, sitting in that first session, I finally felt at home. Nonetheless, the training as a Chaplain was a culture shock. As a Catholic woman, I thought ministry was reserved for priests at the altar and nuns in habits. God had set my sails, though, and I went on to complete three academic degrees and four clinical units, and I became certified in ministry and bereavement.

How did I view these events in terms of my relationship with God? I suppose I could describe it as a "connected distance." I had a sense of separation from God because of my belief that God lived in the heavens while I lived on earth. However, God seemed to be intervening in my life by healing me, leading me toward self-care, and expanding my personal life through education and a call to ministry. Nonetheless, I did struggle in my faith after the marital crisis that wiped me out emotionally. Everything I thought I had learned about God during my spiritual renewal in the late 1970s went out the window, and I started over. For about a year I hardly wanted to speak to God because I was so angry that God had let my marital crisis happen, wreaking havoc in my life.

At this time I learned that every loss is in some way a spiritual crisis, because spirituality is the relationship with something higher than oneself, the self and other. Other relates to people and things both tangible and intangible. The loss of attachments to that which we are in relationship to, and the tearing away that occurs in a loss can create a spiritual crisis. The childhood loss of attachment to my dad created a spiritual crisis of the love relationship value between us and the value of myself. The tearing of the relationship and attachment to Dad and my first husband had a rippling effect on my relationship with God.

During that time of great difficulty, I was invited by an Australian nun to attend a small group for silent prayer. Participation in this small group was my initial introduction to the experience of dialogue with God in stillness. After a period of silence, the nun told us that if we had a question for God, we should ask it in the silence of our hearts and listen to the answer.

I asked God, "Why! Why did you let this happen to me?"

The answer I received was, "There is no power in it."

"No power in it?" I replied. "Look at me! I'm a mess; I can't function." I found this answer quite confusing. In the midst of my pain, the response almost seemed cold.

After that prayer experience, I was angry and wasn't on speaking terms with God for months. However, on another retreat, she talked about coming to God with such "ardor" and persistent desire that God could not refuse to respond. One night I determinedly sat up, refus-

ing to go to bed until I heard from God. After sitting up
practically all night, a peace and sense of presence I had
never known before slowly seeped over my being. *Well,
finally,* I thought, and I went to bed.

God's guiding and assuring grace was beyond my conscious recognition at times when my life seemed unmanageable, yet new paths presented themselves. I seemed to
be disconnected from these happenings, in the sense that
I certainly had not envisioned any of them occurring in
my life. I just seemed to realize myself in circumstances I
had not predicted for myself. For example, during clinical pastoral training I focused on the mental health field
and alcohol and drug addiction, but I ended up spend-
ing eight years as a hospital clinical chaplain. Although
I didn't intend to be part of hospital ministry, it was a
perfect preparation for the end of life care I provided in a
hospice though I did not foresee hospice work.

Now that I am again in transition forty years later,
it is good to remember that in the past, although I was
clueless as to the depth of grace working in my life, I
was, in fact, cooperating with it. Although I argued with
God about going to work, I did it, which helped lift
my depression. Although I was terrified of returning to
school, I found the courage to apply and become a college student. When I became painfully aware that I was
not living the Gospel, I left full-time work to volunteer,
which led me to ministry. Although I had no exposure to
lay women in ministry, I found myself at home in clinical
pastoral ministry.

Although I did not realize it at the time, these desires
for more fulfillment and my courage to step out in unim-

agined directions were signs I was living life in the Spirit.
I surrendered to something greater than myself in times
of misery, discontent, and restlessness; as my own will
softened, God used the opportunity to transition and
transform my life. Everything I had thought and my own
understanding was less than God's vision of what I could
and would accomplish. It is enough, I believe, that we
hope there is a higher being who receives all we surrender in our miseries and despair. Our desires are known
by the One who sees more clearly than we ourselves can
see and responds graciously. I encourage you to believe
that a Spirit of life is working quietly in the darkness at
the center of your own being, bringing about with determined love more than you could ask for or imagine.

My heart is touched over and over by God's quiet,
persistent love and determined assurance that each created life will be given what it needs to accomplish its
unique expression of self. Unlike humans, God does not
need to make a big public acknowledgement about the
mysteries working in us. No—we will experience no
fanfare, no strobe lights flooding the arena, no voices of
angels declaring God's work, no columns of smoke in
the desert or exuberant heavens thundering that God's
hand is at work. The loving, quiet, steadfast grace working from hidden places within the stillness speaks of the
penetrating intimacy with which God works in God's
own creation. Go to the quiet to find the stillness that
speaks your life.

The Ultimate Surrender

It is Wisdom's loving nature to remain hidden; it is faith that allows us to believe she is present. In painful times, acknowledging the presence of Wisdom is difficult. We are such blind creatures when it comes to our spiritual lives. When I was in crisis, I could not see grace at work in my life. I had no awareness of Wisdom's mysteries. I had no concept of love's perseverance and could see no light in my circumstances.

What is it about being in darkness that makes it so tragic? Actually, what is tragic is not the darkness itself but rather our ignorance of the gift the darkness offers. When darkness is embraced, not feared, it eases more peacefully and cooperatively with the new life that is coming—yet, as from a womb, we struggle. In not understanding the need to accept what is, I created more suffering for myself. I was often frustrated by my lack of control, my bumbling attempts to manage life, and my limitations. It pleases me now and reassures me that despite myself Something Greater was actively, mysteriously caring for me in the midst of life's complexities and impossibilities. My human ego fought surrender to something greater than myself, even as I desired it, which illustrates the struggle between the human and spiritual aspects of my being.

My years of struggle with life's difficulties were intertwined with my humanity. Even though people, books, teachings, education—you name it—tried to tell me how to avoid this entanglement, for some reason I had to live in the midst of it before I could gain the insight to step out of it and live life differently. I suppose I had to slosh around in the muck for a while before I truly desired to be free of it. I attribute silent prayer as the place where change began to happen within.

Because of my unresolved childhood grief my life was absorbed by my mind and the way it functioned, which kept me from being aware of my own soul. The religious education I received during my childhood, with its foundation of sin, guilt, and the need to earn God's favor and love, also robbed me of my awareness of the truth of my soul. These teachings gave me a sense of separateness from God. Basically, I was taught that I had to be good, and then when I died I could go to heaven and be with God. It takes God's patient, persistent grace to dislodge the many religious teachings that contradict the experience of God's sovereign truth and love. In stillness—in God's ever-watchful, loving presence—I slogged through my mind's memories and unfounded beliefs and experienced God's love. Truth dislodges mistruths of interpretation, perceptions, and beliefs that are an inevitable consequence of being born on the earth. We are raised in a world of a non-pure environment of mistruth, human perceptions, and religion's good but sometimes misguided intentions.

It is in the stillness of Presence that we absorb hidden grace. It is the workings of grace that begin to loosen the hold of untruth in our mind as the experience of God releases them. The Spirit of truth is for each of us and is within us. When we experience God's revealing grace, untruth's thoughts, reasoning, interpretations, false beliefs, and false identity are dislodged and turn to ashes. We see more clearly how false perceptions affected our life. Considering the depth of what I found in the darkness, I don't know what, other than the Spirit of God, could have enlightened those areas.

We are raised in environments that condition our relationships with our family, our social contacts, our community, and our self. Years ago, as I began to believe in the unconditional love of God, I knew that I would spend the rest of my life growing into the acceptance of unconditional love. I also knew I would not find this knowledge outside of myself, in other people, because we share human nature's imperfections. Deep within each of us is a place where we yearn for that which no human can provide. That yearning is only satisfied in the connected relationship with the One from whom we have come. We come to know that there is no separation from our Creator. It is only in a relationship consummated in awareness that I have found the exquisite love that nothing and no one in this universe can provide, and I do not believe that this love can be experienced anywhere except deep within each person.

Now that I have experienced the unconditional love of God, I know it is this love that is the greatest desire of the heart and the ultimate satisfaction of the soul. How did I go from being a disturbed woman who sat in a church once a week to living consciously in peace? How did my soul come to know the ultimate life experience of God's love? How did this great distance get shortened to the extent that each breath of my existence is the very breath of God?

In the early 1990s I was nearing the end of my education, and graduation was approaching. A friend and I decided to take a cruise, using the money I had saved for my education, I might add.

"Oh, go on the cruise," she reasoned. "Get a school loan."

During the cruise, while others complained about the weather, I was exhilarated by the dark sky with its ominous, threatening clouds. At 2:00 a.m. the wind created fifteen-foot waves, and the black depths of the sea beckoned. Having the deck to myself, I tried to figure out how to get over the high sides of the ship to slip into the inviting depths of the sea.

I had just discovered a ladder and intended to climb over the railing when that familiar whisper interrupted my plan: *You may not be able to do everything, but there is something you can do.* This thought cut through my plans to jump ship, leaving me instead to wonder what that *something* might be. In the midst of my hopelessness, it was a spark of hope. I returned to my cabin and went to bed. It is amazing how the power of the Spirit of truth can wipe away in a mere breath the compelling mental obsessions that are beyond our control. When God speaks, what is *not* of God dissipates to the nothing that it is.

At that time I was at the mercy of depression—its oscillations from hope to despair, its ebb and flow patterns, its unpredictability, and the way it undermined my confidence and self-esteem even in what would seem the best of times. I was accomplishing all I had set out to accomplish, yet my spirit was heavy with depression. Depression's power is insidious when we are unaware of and unfamiliar with its patterns and characteristics as they work in us.

I had completed my master's degree in pastoral ministry and was in the process of becoming certified as a chaplain. It was at this time that I self-diagnosed my depression. I was working at a state mental institution and was asked to create a dual-diagnosis program for alcohol and drug abuse and depression. As I read the *Diagnostic and Statistical Manual* used by mental health professionals to diagnos mental illness, I was shocked to realize that I had every single one of the characteristics of a person with depression.

During marital counseling I had been told that I had "reactive depression" because of the problems in my marriage. The major depressive episodes I experienced when I was thirteen years old and during my crisis in the 1980s, not to mention the suicidal ideation sandwiched in between, were never addressed as a clinical problem. If depression is initially treated, there is less chance of re-occurrence. If depression is left untreated, more episodes with more frequency can develop. Mine had gone untreated since childhood. My depression was at the point I would drop into a depression with just a negative thought.

In looking at the characteristics of depression, I realized I had never known life outside of depression. I had no life comparisons. I decided to seek an accurate diagnosis from a psychiatrist, who confirmed the depression and explained that it originated in childhood. Before we could explore its beginnings, I had another episode. I couldn't get out of bed or shower without assistance. I called the doctor, who prescribed my first medication for depression.

Within five days, it was as if I was living on a new planet; the trees had leaves, and the sky was blue. The near debilitating fatigue was gone. I came home after a full day at work with enough energy to get dinner on the table and to do a couple of loads of laundry. I had a sense of well-being, of personal value. I felt happier. I wasn't as irritable. Depression's anxiety was gone. I was feeling more confident at work. I did not wake up in the morning with the customary thought, "Oh, gawd, another day." I wondered, *Is this how normal people feel?* I felt wonderful. My psychiatrist suggested that my life must have been like walking upstream in waders filled with water. I explained that it was more like walking on the bottom of a pool in the deep end. The doctor noted how I lived life on a day-to-day basis through sheer willpower while I was depressed. People with depression rely heavily on developing a strong will—the will to get up, the will to eat, and the will to move through the day. Living through willpower could earn us academy awards for how well people with depression fake living.

For about seven years I had no major depressive episodes on the medication. During that period my husband decided to stop going to counseling, despite my concern that it would jeopardize our marriage if he quit and that we would fall back into old patterns. When he said he had made his decision, I knew the end of our marriage was inevitable. I had now been in Al-Anon for about fourteen years, and I accepted that all that could be done had been done, and that I had nothing left to give him. We divorced in 1995. I remember how amazed I was that I went through managing the divorce without a depressive episode.

Years later, employed as a hospital clinical chaplain, the position became more demanding, and then the chaplain with whom I had shared responsibility for the crisis care units left in 1998, the year I remarried. I told my supervisor and peers that I was unable to meet the demands of the high crisis responsibilities, that I was experiencing burnout, and that I was having trouble with depression.

However, I was expected to continue on as usual. I started receiving disciplinary write-ups, and I again explained to the supervisor that I was having classic symptoms of burnout and depression and that I needed help, not disciplinary action. I sought assistance through the Employees Assistance Program and continued to see my psychiatrist as I tried to cope by doing everything I knew about self-care. All my efforts were to no avail.

In January 2000, I crashed with a debilitating depression requiring me to take family leave from work. I returned to work after 120 days of medical leave, but I still was not up to full capacity. My doctor had increased the levels of my medications and tried to ease me back into work, and the hospital allowed me to work flexible hours. However, the supervisor continued to interact with me in a punitive manner, and the point came where I would not meet with him unless someone else was present. After three months, I knew my mental health recovery would be jeopardized if I continued to work with this man. The human resources department was no help, and the hospital hotline never called back. I resigned and immediately was hired as a part-time chaplain in another hospital's hospice program.

My work environment was much improved, but I was covering two positions and the part-time hours were inadequate to meet the demands. My anxiety was increasing. At an annual visit to my primary doctor, she asked me if I was having trouble with anxiety. I said I was and attributed it to work. She suspected the anxiety was due to one of the medications that increases anxiety and took me off one of the two antidepressants the psychiatrist had prescribed. That change helped with the anxiety, but the medication was now non-therapeutic for the depression. Within a few weeks, I relapsed into my deepest depression. At the time I was on the wait list for a doctor that my social worker thought could better manage the antidepressants. My appointment was not for another 30 days, though. It would only be in hindsight that we would realize an unforeseen implosion had been on the horizon; taking the antidepressant for over seven years, the bottom was falling out and becoming ineffective, my body chemistry was changing due to menopause, coupled with increasing stress at work.

On December 26, 2002, as I was driving home from work in increasing mental anguish, I felt like my mind was screaming. The house seemed like it had too much space, so I went to my quilt room where I usually find the craft or music comforting. I could not distract my mind from its screaming without words. My husband came home from work and seeing me sitting there asked how my day had been.

"Not good," I said.

"Do you want to talk about it?" he asked.

I shook my head. I couldn't talk about my day or what my mind was doing. It was cold outside, and my mind became taken up with how I wished he would leave the house so I could go outside in the freezing weather. I knew where I could hide in our back acreage where I could freeze to death before anyone found me. The room then became too overwhelming, and I moved to the closet shutting the door for complete darkness. All senses became overwhelmed, and everything was too much. Later he found me curled up on the closet floor, unable to move or respond to him; I was practically catatonic.

For the first time I was hospitalized for depression, and suicide precautions were initiated. My medications were doubled. The day before I was to be discharged I hid in the dark bathroom of my room, trying to figure out how I could kill myself. Because the towel bars were sealed, I could not get a towel or piece of clothing over it to hang myself. I thought of banging my head into the tile wall, but I knew that wouldn't kill me. How frustrated and hopeless I felt.

I reached the most helpless point of my life and prayed, "Lord, not even the love of my husband or my children is enough to make me want to take another breath, but I can't stop myself from breathing. If I am to live, you will have to do life in me." A peace washed over me and stilled my anguish. Soon afterward, a nurse found me. I could barely respond to her, but I asked if she would pray for me. She held my hand. While she prayed silently, I heard the Voice say, *You will be delivered.* From what I would be delivered, I did not know.

I was discharged the next day. When I returned home, I knew I needed to do life differently, though I had no idea what that meant. I did know I should turn to what had always been at the root of my life's changes in the past. I returned to meditation.

DIVORCING THE MIND

Fully and completely surrendering one's known life can be like finding oneself suddenly plunked down on a new, barren planet with no obvious signs of life support. When we completely surrender, all is fully and freely given to us. However, at first we aren't aware of this gift because we are still attached to what our mind says and haven't yet learned how to live from the perspective of our spirit soul.

One day in the 1970s, as I entered the dining room from the kitchen of my house, I passed from one room to another, not only physically but metaphorically, in a spiritual sense. I suddenly became conscious of the many times I had tried working things out as *I* saw them, only to find I was in the wrong ball field altogether. Chuckling to myself (although the waywardness of my will wasn't particularly funny with regard to the consequences), I decided there and then, standing in my dining room, to let God have a go at my life. The decision made, I returned to my household tasks. And thus, between the kitchen and the hallway, with a moment's pause for awareness and surrender in the midst of my busyness, my life changed and I embarked on a new path, in a new spirit.

It was only months later that I began to realize that God took my almost flippant relinquishment during that moment and blessed it abundantly. Whereas humans measure love and dole it out sparingly, with God love is always abundant. When I made my simple decision to surrender, it was as if I was standing in the Sahara Desert and leaned down with a pair of tweezers to move a single grain of sand. Although the desert had been changed and was no longer the same, the change could not be detected by me or anyone else.

The grace of God at work in my spontaneous moment of surrender in my dining room was no less disproportionate to the grace at work in my excruciating surrender on the bathroom floor of the psychiatric hospital. Grace is grace. It is the loving compassion that is ready to be poured out when we relinquish self-management and give God permission to give what would be given. Our will and desire to either hang on or let go—the decision to pursue our own way of being or to relinquish it—is our greatest power, influencing the release of true life working in us. However, we are oblivious to the fact that we are not the initiators of life or the maintainers of it.

I was raised to be strong, to exert my will, and to work at life. However, I was never taught the spiritual reality that our true life is not centered in our physical realities, but is centered in the Lord and that God is the initiator of all life. Many people have the perception that God created the heavens and the earth, and that creation stopped at that point. The reality is that God's creation is ongoing and has eternal momentum. God is still in the act of creating, and what is being created includes my life.

It was only when I reached my mental, emotional, and physical capacity and confronted the brink of my human limitation and endurance that I cried out that if I was to live, God would have to do life in me. I had thought my only options were to live life as I had known it in depression or ceasing to live at all. I did not realize that the fullness of life, the truth of what it is to live, would be revealed only if I let go and relinquished myself to a greater being. I could not hold onto anything. Although I had nothing to lose in relinquishment, neither did I believe I had anything to gain. I had only known life as it related to my human experience, and I wanted nothing to do with it. I was done—so done.

Let me take a moment here to speak to those who have experienced the tragedy of losing a loved one to suicide. I hope that what I can tell you about living with depression might provide some insight and perhaps a bit of balm for your anguish.

For me, being afflicted with depression was like having four separate entities operating within myself. First was the physical, public self that went to work and functioned by carrying out the requirements of the day through sheer willpower and determination. Although depression robbed me of the desire to engage in life, I developed the ability to function publicly in response to life's demands by summoning my will and putting one foot in front of the other with determination.

The second entity operating within me was centered in my heart, where love for my husband, children, and grandchildren was expressed and experienced in a good, loving environment. I was authentically loving and caring with the patients and families I served in the hospital and hospice. However, what others cannot see in a person who is depressed is the lack of love for *oneself,* the void and absence of self-esteem, and the pervasive sense of not fitting in the world, of not belonging, of being unable to attach to life and the world around you.

How many times have we heard persons who lost a loved one to suicide ask, "Didn't he love us?" "Didn't she know how much we love her?" and "How could she/he do this?" But speaking for myself, and perhaps for others, when we are in the despairing depths of depression, it's not as if we are considering the love we have received or have given to others and are intentionally dismissing it. In the midst of whatever else is going on in the mind (which, by the way, was the third entity operating inside me), the mind absorbs and distorts the existence or value of love. Love goes to a place that just does not seem to be part of the present moment's thinking and distorted reasoning. The mind is beyond what survivors see as simple, rationalizing love. At the time a person attempts suicide, the mind and heart cannot reach each other. *Depression is not rational.*

Do you remember me speaking of my ruminations when I was thirteen years old that no one loved me? Those thoughts weren't true, for I knew my grandmother loved me, and yet that knowledge was totally obliterated in the process of my mind overtaking my heart. Having remarried in 1998, I was living in a very good marriage— actually, one made in heaven—and yet the relationship was not enough to overcome the anguish filling my mind, which was all-encompassing and obliterated the value of love. Had I experienced times in the past when my awareness of love and thoughts of others were able to overpower my mind's obsession with leaving the world? Yes. During my episode in the psychiatric hospital, however, I was not able to retrieve those thoughts and factor them in. I was consumed with wanting to get out of the world, and at the time, leaving the world seemed to make good sense.

Many people say that depression and suicide is an act of anger. In so far as anger is attached to pain and it is human nature to try to stop pain, then yes, I would say that anger was a part of my suicide plans, but it was hidden from my conscious mind. When I attempted suicide at age thirteen, I do not remember having any feelings of anger or a desire for retaliation. I do remember having the mental obsession that no one loved me. Neither was I able to think and remember about how much I was loved unconditionally by my grand-mother. Suicide simply seemed the only way out of pain.

And what of the soul, which was the fourth entity operating inside me? Remember, I had a history of experiencing moments of spiritual consolation, of sensing God's presence. In my social circle, I was known as a woman of faith. I suspect that people who are able to resist committing suicide because they believe it is a sin are in the same place mentally as those who are able to resist carrying out their suicide plans because of love for their family.

I believe the difference between those who are and are not able to resist the compulsion to kill themselves is the depth of depression's hold on their mind at the time. Based on my experience, I believe a moment can come when the mind has no capacity for the natural reasoning that would allow preservation of self. It is important to remember that when one is in a state to the depth to which depression can take you, one sees no reason to preserve the self—just the opposite. This compulsion to end one's life absolutely goes against the self-survival instincts that are ingrained deep within our natural being.

To have being is to have the freedom and ability to be connected to one's soul spirit while living as a human. To live a fulfilling life as a human, the self must be valued and connected. In my very amateur way of understanding my own relationship within my whole being, I would say there was a disconnect between my physical self, my mind, my heart, and my soul. In a sense, they were working as separate, incongruent, disharmonious aspects of my personhood—and they weren't getting along.

My journey to wholeness through meditation began when these four entities started to recognize each other. When I discovered the disharmonies and incongruence within me, when I became aware of the pain and miseries within my own thinking, I found the freedom to choose the experience of true self in the depth of the soul. Peace of mind had nothing to do with what was going on *outside* myself. It was what was hidden within the depth of my soul that needed to experience love and acceptance from within. Through the experience of divine love, the four wayward entities were able to become a cohesive unit of well-being.

It was in the soul's workings that the power of love opened up my awareness of the existence of life on another level of reality. I no longer wanted life as I had known it. Through the dining room of divine sustenance I was able to disengage from a busy, almost driven life of external action in which I overcompensated for what I thought I lacked. I could also recognize and disengage from characteristics of depression and moved into a new life in spirit and in joy.

Depression was the avenue of human limitation that ultimately led me to new life. I believe that any human circumstance or situation can be an avenue to new life when it leads a person to surrender to the actual Creator of life. I came to this belief only in hindsight, as I realized how my human mind was connected to what I could interpret and perceive of life. I now believe that any obsession or addiction to gratifying the senses has the potential to lead to new life when its miseries foster surrender to the Supreme. Alcoholics Anonymous thrives on this principle of a Higher Power managing what we cannot manage. Surrender works for AA. Surrender worked for my addiction to nicotine. Surrender for depression seemed to work on the same principal.

What I write in this book is a deep personal experience of the power of the first three steps in the twelve-step program: acknowledging I am powerless over that which I no longer want in my life, asking God to restore my sanity to free my mind from its entanglements, and turning my will and life over to God. The same powerful practice has been found to be successful in overcoming addictions to food, sex, drugs, gambling, shopping, workaholism, and the like.

In naming these addictions and discovering the power of the twelve-step program to overcome them, I do not digress from my story, as I soon discovered in my decision to do life differently. My first decision was to return to a practice that had helped me initiate life changes in the past—prayer. I began each day in meditation. Although it certainly wasn't funny at the time, I would later tell someone that people in a state of depression are half-way to a state of contemplation, because our minds are numb anyway. In addition, I read that depression can be reframed and considered to be spiritual stillness or solitude. The reframing of my mental illness as an opportunity for the spiritual practice of solitude and meditation somewhat eased the burden of it.

Resigning from my job after I was hospitalized was the impetus to discovering my workaholism. Only when I did not have the prop of work did the underlying panic and anxiety that were attached to my practice of identifying with work as self raise their true colors. If one can pause, or stop the unwanted behavior, and move instead into stillness to quiet the mind, the inner voices, tapes, and mind's conditioning are made conscious. Meeting one's own mind takes courage.

I did not venture into meditation alone, but with the companionship of the journaling process to help me express my thoughts and feelings. Along with meditation, journaling had seen me through my marriage crisis and subsequent divorce. Journaling accompanied me on my visits to my social worker, Nancy J. Later Nancy would say how much the process of meditation and journaling enhanced the therapeutic process. I offer heartfelt gratitude for all therapists who accept spirituality as a process companion and enhancement to well-being and the search for wholeness.

Depending on my state of mind, I might start my daily quiet time with journaling to empty myself of the angst and anxiety that was overwhelming me. After quieting myself through journaling, I could still my mind to meditate. Sometimes I started with meditation, and after my mind stilled, I discovered hidden feelings, thoughts, and beliefs that dramatically affected the quality of my life. Journaling helped me more fully address what was hidden.

Eventually I turned to other resources as well. Reading and searching were leading me in directions I previously had not explored spiritually. One of the most significant turning points of recovering my mental health was when I read the straightforward statement, "You are not your mind," from Eckhart Tolle's *The Power of Now*. I am not my mind? Then what am I? It was as if someone had taken an eraser and wiped the board clean.

This idea that I am not my mind was then reinforced in many different types of reading materials, from spiritual to secular. I learned that my mind is a functional organ and I am more than that. *The mind is a wonderful tool and a terrible master*. We are body, mind and spirit; the greatest of these is the spiritual self. We are of the divine. The mind is for the purpose of interpreting, perceiving, and analyzing what the senses and the intellect present. We are in control of the mind through our will and choice.

To believe that one's self is the mind, and to follow its impulses and thoughts as fact without questioning its interpretations, makes for a miserable existence. The mind does not know the difference between what is imaged and what is actually experienced. I had come to hate my mind for all the miseries it caused by not being smart enough and by causing my depression. What I was reading was telling me that I am separate from the mind, and my true self could manage and influence my mind's workings and functions. *This understanding was critical to changing my relationship with myself.*

This discovery of the role of my mind had a significant impact on my relationship with depression and how I saw myself. I believed all my thoughts and assumed these thoughts were who I was. Therapy helped me begin to disentangle my true self from the characteristics of depression. It was not that I had below-average intelligence, as I had come to believe in elementary school. Rather, depression hampers the ability to focus, memorize, or concentrate, and the ability to analyze is impaired. It is no wonder I had difficulty in school, as I was hampered in my ability to meet the education system's demands. Because I also found it very difficult to make decisions and to follow through on ideas, I thought I had a weak character. However, these characteristics also are a consequence of depression and are not the result of a lack of character.

The realization of how the mind functions to safeguard the ego for the sake of self-preservation helped me to understand how entangled my identity had become in the work ethic. As a child, my mind interpreted my father's absence as meaning that his work was more important than me. Believing my own thoughts led to a painful and quite depressed life of grieving the loss of my attachment to my dad. This grief significantly affected my quality of life. Now, as an adult, I somberly realized that my entire experience and consequences of that loss of attachment had been based on a child's interpretation and perception.

Of course, a child does not question what he or she thinks. As an adult, it was time to become vigilantly aware of my thinking, to question the truth of my thoughts and the resulting feelings, and to notice how they affected my well-being. The spiritual values of loving and forgiving oneself helped my soul bring balance to my wayward mind. I was finding myself to be a steward of my thoughts and not a victim of them.

As I became aware of how attached I was to believing what my mind told me, I also became more aware of my yearnings and desires. I can't begin to explain the panic and anxiety I was experiencing by not working. It was cold-turkey withdrawal—anguishing and disorienting. By becoming more mindful of my thoughts and not attaching to them, I realized, too, that my yearnings and desires were also false because they were attached to what was a distorted sense of self. Work had become my value and identity. My anxiety was a result of *de*taching myself from the practice of *a*ttaching myself to something that was really a false self. This shocking new awareness was also liberating my mind. I could turn to my authentic self. By detaching from what was a false self, I began turning and attaching to what spiritual readings suggested was my true self—a living entity created by the good and loving Supreme Creator.

I am not my mind. I am not what my mind thinks. I am not what the world tells me I am. I am created by something greater than myself. I am of that from which I came. And through it all, I was having another experience I could not deny. In the stillness, in the quiet, I was being loved unconditionally. The spiritual poverty I felt as a young child because I believed no one loved me was becoming satisfied.

What had been the yearnings and desires of my mind and heart were becoming ashes, disintegrating in importance and reality. I began to yearn more and more for the spiritual truths that were awakening me to my value by virtue of nothing more than my created existence. It was a process of detaching from the workings of the mind and attaching to the awareness of my soul as the truth of my "I am." In looking at what gave me pleasure, superficial though it remained, I recognized my yearnings and desires as being the dissatisfaction that it was. I began to disengage from unhappiness about what was lacking in my life, the comparisons that ached for more, and the sense of scarcity that said I didn't have what I needed. In looking at not working in a different way, I could see that I had been withdrawing from the ego recognition that my work positions provided. I no longer needed that and saw it for the false entanglement that it was. I was loved and valued, even if I never did another thing but sit on the couch and watch Oprah! That devouring tiger of work was falling apart—and I wasn't.

I made the decision to divorce myself from my attachment to the workings of my mind and attach myself to something healthier for my well-being. Spirituality is the relationship to something greater than one's self, self, and other. I began to look for spiritual resources within the truth of my soul. Less and less was I attached and attentive to the workings of the mind. In essence, I didn't "mind" what it was doing. I wasn't cooperating with the thoughts, and left alone, the mind was getting quieter and less demanding. I loved the scene in the movie *A Beautiful Mind* in which John Nash, who suffered from schizophrenia, realized that the people he was seeing and the voices he was hearing were not real and he made a conscious choice to ignore them. I, too, ignored the mind, but tended the *soul*.

LIBERATING THE SOUL

It is not uncommon to hear personal stories of recovery from depression that is rooted in unresolved grief. Grief represents the impact of the loss that has occurred, and mourning—which is the expression of the grief—is part of the healing process. Unresolved grief also can contribute to physical illness. In my case, unresolved grief was a definite factor in my tenuous mental health and resulting depression.

Mindfulness, meditation, relaxation, and stress reduction are becoming recognized avenues for recovery from and management of depression and anxiety. Journaling also is a valued and helpful tool in the mourning process because it dismisses the element of *linear* time and allows thoughts and feelings to become conscious in the present moment. When I read my journals I was surprised to find that, at times, I had written in the voice of a child, as if no linear time had passed.

Because I attempted to write about my experiences with honesty and authenticity, my journals consisted of uncensored and unedited expressions of the thoughts and feelings that were alive in my memories. I wrote about the Father/Daughter Banquet that affected me so deeply when I was eight years old. I wrote about how I felt abandoned by my dad and his work ethic and how work became my only attachment to him.

I wrote about my relationship to work and the entanglement of my identity and value in my work, including the panic and anxiety I felt when I was not working. I wrote about my resulting loss of purpose and meaning when I couldn't work. I wrote about my loneliness as a child, about my teachers and school, and about what it was like to grow up in my family. I wrote and wrote, vented and cried, and said everything a child is not allowed to say and everything that is socially unacceptable for an adult to say. I heard and accepted my own voice.

I began to hear another voice in the stillness—a voice not my own. It came to me with compassion, love, wisdom, understanding, and encouragement. It clearly accepted me with no condemnation of anything I freely expressed. The Voice taught me about thoughts and feelings, heart and soul, human nature, the workings of the mind and the spiritual path as a new way of life. And always present was the invitation to move away from the futile ways of the world and come to a deeper way of knowing.

Instead of avoiding my thoughts and feelings, the Spirit encouraged, "It is better to enter the darkness than to let darkness enter you." It taught me that to explore memories of experiences with feelings attached to them is like walking into a room with photos hanging on unseen lines of energy. If I rushed through these memories they would tear at me like paper cuts and be quite painful. However, if I moved slowly as I met these memories, I would be aware, I would remember, and I would feel the feelings, but I could let them slide past me without causing me harm. They were experiences. They were not *me*.

I continued to stroll through these memories as they presented themselves and discovered that the most difficult of them demanded many visits before I could ease the pain associated with them. As my mind remembered, my soul had to realize how I had attached myself, my value, and my identity to the experience. For example, as an eight-year-old child, I thought that work was more important than *me*. As an adult, I finally understood that my child's mind had done just what a mind typically does when the ego is threatened—it made assumptions and played its own interpretation of the event over and over, until that interpretation became entangled in my own value of myself.

After *dis*engaging from my mind, I was able to *en*gage the spiritual part of myself. Disentangling myself from my mind was a gentle process as I realized the human nature and spiritual core of my being. This process of growing in awareness helped me heal. In the past, I had been bonded to my thoughts, not my soul. I rarely gave thought to my soul, save for wondering whether it was good enough to merit salvation at death. My focus was always on the afterlife. Now I discovered that what was happening in my spiritual life *was* the actual loving experience of the divine in the present. I felt a Presence in the quiet, and I experienced intimate moments of reassuring love and compassion. God never, ever brought up sin or faults; I only experienced acceptance and life wisdom. I had been in bondage to, in relationship with, and attached to my mind and was totally ignorant of the Presence within my soul and the source of my breath's very existence.

God must see us compassionately as lost within our thinking mind. God sees that we are caught in our material nature and understands that at our soul level we do not actually desire that for which we *think* we are yearning. Once we see clearly and are free, we choose the ultimate good. No longer blind, we yearn for more to satisfy the soul and seek God through prayer, loving ourselves, and loving others.

Do you remember in my prayer of surrender in the hospital that I didn't want to take another breath? Now, through breath awareness meditation, breath has transcended my previously unconscious need to become the very breath of my existence. My breath is connected to my life Source, and I no longer take it for granted as an involuntary physical rhythm. As a child, my mantra was that no one loved me. Now, I find in the stillness a loving Presence I experience so profoundly that there is absolutely no question I am loved unconditionally. Magnanimous love takes whatever human poverty we offer, fills it, and transforms it to love's satisfaction. The child who thought herself stupid received words of healing wisdom of which the mystics have written. The woman who thought her identity resided in work has found that she is a manifested thought of God and that her soul was actually conceived in God's love.

"Who made you?" the Baltimore Catechism asked. As a child, with the mind's linear thinking, I perceived this as God is there and created me here. Now in my developing spirituality, I answer from the experience of deeper truth: God made me. I am of the Divine. I am in the Divine and the Divine is within me. John 14 beautifully describes this truth. And what is the first commandment? "We are to love God with our whole might and mind and heart and love our neighbor as ourselves." To actually live through the wilderness process—to liberate ourselves from our bondage to this world and live a spiritual life—requires wading through the false self that is attached to our false existence created in the mind.

I surrendered to life's miseries and found new life hidden within life as I had known it. My ultimate goal was to surrender my attachment to the workings of the mind and the workings of the world. By detaching and letting go of attachments to work, awards, education, and certifications—to all false identifications—I was able to free-fall into the truth of my actual being. It was like leaning back into God, truth would act like a sieve freeing me of what is not true within my concept of myself.

My desires and yearnings toward life were quite misplaced. Through the human environments constructed by my parents, teachers, and society, I was taught what they thought was the truth, but a much deeper truth is mysteriously hidden behind the mind. We come from a loving Being, we live in the presence of a loving Being, and a loving Being is found within the soul, the quietest of places within our being. My times of meditation, journaling, and wisdom writings enlightened my way, but my openness to new spiritual searches was merely receptivity to what grace brought to my path of recovery. God initiates the invitation; it is our choice to respond.

If I had remained on what I thought was the only right course, on a path I myself defined, I would have missed cooperating with the Spirit of life. Although you may feel like you are stepping off a cliff or out of a plane at thirty thousand feet when you surrender desperate situations, you will be caught and guided softly to a safe landing. I encourage you to enter your darkness and to choose, accept, and explore your difficult times, believing that a Spirit of goodness is orchestrating your un-choreographed dance with life.

I share with you the wise voice that accompanied me through years of depression's darkness, fear, anxiety, panic, and misplaced self-loathing: "Stick with the process. Stick with the process!", my husband would encourage. I won't tell you how I retorted to that encouragement, but I will tell you it is true. It's all a process, a spiritual process, a path to new life. When I surrendered to what I could not tolerate, a spiritual process was hidden beneath the working of my mind, in the hidden places of my soul, within my true self.

It was not without kicking and screaming that I jerked free of all that entangled my mind. While knowing in the hospital that I would be delivered, I could not possibly know what I needed to be delivered from. I needed liberation from the entanglements of the conditioned mind attached superficially to the surface of this world. It takes nothing short of courage to face the wilderness process, but once you begin to get the feel of Wisdom's small liberating movements encouraging you along the way, you begin to understand that you are in this world but not of it—that your true self is the very manifestation of a Supreme Being—that you are fully delivered and liberated to new life.

I went looking for peace of mind and discovered I did not need to leave this world to find the peace I sought. I found the intimate experience of the divine in the stillness, behind the thinking. My mind was once a larger entity than my soul. Now my soul is the governor of my mind. Is a thought nonjudgmental, loving, kind, and accepting? Then it is in the realm of the Divine, the spiritual life, soul. I choose that. Detect and resist any negative thought that would not be of the Divine's way of thinking. I am aware of my thoughts. I do not attach myself to a thought. I remain conscious of the truth of myself, my own source of being, though I cannot rise much above the realization on my own—it can only be revealed. How could I know more of myself or life other than being of love, loved, and loving? Nothing else has any permanence or is worthy of attention.

A quiet mind does not need to expend wasted energy on worry, on questioning one's own value and worth, or even on one's purpose and meaning. For one who is in the true stream of what is life-giving, life is energized with enthusiasm for what will come, and the joy of anticipation bubbles over into quiet pools of waiting. At the same time, as each day unfolds I am connected to Something Greater than me who is revealing the Something More my spirit longed for. Remaining attached to the divine source and fountain of life, I know life here as it is meant to be lived will not disappoint me, for disappointment is a working of the mind, and I don't live there anymore. I've been delivered from the working of my mind and I now live in awareness of the Presence in my soul.

Having encountered a healing and compassionate spiritual presence within the recesses of my soul, I came to believe that I would experience complete healing only through a spiritual pathway. It helped to stay connected to the value of the spiritual path when my therapist supported its value. For example, once when I relapsed, my doctor asked me if I had been doing anything previously that I was no longer doing. *Meditation* was my response.

"Well," he said, "go meditate and come back in six weeks, and we'll see how you're doing." When I returned to the spiritual path, I re-stabilized. I now have no inclination to set aside my daily spiritual practices. I realize that *the quality of my life is within every breath and is linked to the conscious awareness of the Source of all life.*

Just as I could not have managed my depression without outside help, I could not have healed from depression without inside help. I monitor certain spiritual principles that are vital for my well-being. Without a doubt, the primary practice is my commitment and faithfulness to myself and God through daily prayer and meditation. By enhancing my conscious contact with God, and by acknowledging the true source of my life, I cooperate with living freely the life that is available to me. I have a sacred space in the corner of my home where I sit every day open to my ongoing spiritual pathway and the living of my unique life, while attached to the Source of all life.

God honors our faithfulness. On one occasion, I judged my prayer time to be of poor quality because I couldn't quiet my mind. My thoughts seemed to bounce around like an activated pinball machine. In exasperation, I remarked, "Well, that wasn't worth much," and I went to get a cup of coffee. What followed created a deep impression that God hears every thought. I sat down to do some spiritual reading and let out a sigh, but it extended to the point that I could not inhale! My exhalation was long, slow, deep, and drawn out. Then my breath continued to exhale to the point that I felt like my lungs were collapsing or they could be pulled from my chest. My eyes opened wide with the sensation of having my life breath drawn from me, but I was not afraid of dying. I felt, instead, a trusting abandonment to that which could pull my life back into Itself. I remember thinking, *if you want me now, take me. I don't mind coming home.* At the same time my mind was filled with the realization that the quality of prayer cannot be judged. By virtue of our faithfulness, prayers are not to be judged. Prayers are the breath of God life in us. *God is breathing us.* At understanding this, my breath returned to normal, but my perspective on prayer as subject to criticism was forever changed. While there is no room for judgment of prayer, after months of contemplative prayer, one may consider such questions as; Am I more patient? Am I more loving? Am I more forgiving? Am I less fearful?

I have spoken of my time in the proverbial wilderness, where I slowly came to a conscious awareness of the workings of my mind and soul spirit. I allowed my memories to surface naturally as they were triggered by my illness or by an event in the day. To illustrate my new attitude toward detaching myself from life events, I will borrow a metaphor from the book *Mindfulness Through Depression* by Mark Williams, John Teasdale, Zindel Segal, and Jon Kabat-Zinn: Life is like a silent film, for which we provide the voice script—the commentary.

Here is how I changed the script: First, paying attention to the memories so they could heal, I observed my place in the context of the memory as a child or an adult. Second, I rewitnessed the thoughts and feelings and observed that the interpretations or perceptions attached to the events were the workings of the mind, not facts. Third, I determined appropriate options; perhaps I only needed to be compassionate and understanding, because I was vulnerable at the time of the experience. Perhaps I needed to forgive my own interpretations, perceptions, assumptions, and the resulting beliefs, values, attitudes, or behaviors that caused me additional grief. Often I needed to forgive others.

By owning the responsibility of my reactions within the memory, I shared in the outcome. For example, my Dad was responsible for choosing to work on the night of the biggest event of my life when I was eight years old. In returning to that memory as an adult, I could move beyond the hurt and rejection to acknowledge the perspective of a man who had the responsibility of providing shelter, food, and clothing for nine children. By examining the memory as an adult, I could view the perceptions I had as a child and the resulting grief that remained hidden deep within me with sensitivity and compassion.

Forgiveness is the humus, the ground of healing. Forgiveness facilitates the awareness of humanity as a whole and the vulnerability and fragility of the human individual. We all share this world experience with its pain and difficulties. Forgiveness is acceptance of humanity's shared dilemma and its critical need for compassion. In that respect, I have come to greatly appreciate the Buddhist spiritual exercise of *tonglen*, referred to in Pema Chödrön's book, *When Things Fall Apart*. Tonglen is a practice of mindfulness that enhances the ability to be fully aware of the present moment. It provides a way to manage hurtful events as they occur, and it also helps heal painful memories when they get triggered.

To practice tonglen, when aware of being hurt, first acknowledge what the event feels like and allow compassion for yourself. The next step is to expand loving awareness toward others in the community and the world who have experienced the same thing. Circling back, you seek to embrace in thoughtful compassion those who hurt you by what they said or did, recognizing that they, too, have suffered and are expressing their unresolved pain. After accepting the event and surrounding it with compassion, you can decide on the appropriate response from the heart, rather than retaliating in reaction to the pain, as the ego/mind would have you do.

Pausing to choose compassion engages the intellect and the will in an effort to move from the mind to the heart. I have found that tonglen is a liberating tool for dealing with memories and the challenges of daily living. It allows us to hold our own life and the life of others in the light of love's compassion, which we ourselves have received from God. The natural working of stillness helps us to see light and love's embrace, which allow memories to surface from dark places. One then can forgive and embrace oneself and others who are participating in the silent film of our life. Tonglen allows rescripting of both memory and the present, which creates a more peaceful world for ourselves and others.

I had to put tonglen into practice at an event in my home. My husband, who is a very kind and thoughtful fellow, was on the phone negotiating his highly anticipated visit of his two out-of-town nieces–for the same weekend I was to give a retreat! After a bit of three-way conversation, I talked to the niece directly to explain the dilemma. She understood what it takes to prepare for houseguests *and* a weekend retreat, so we talked of another date. Relieved, I handed the phone back to Hubby, who said to her, "Go ahead and come. I'll take care of everything." I'm thinking, *Yeah, right...*

I began to *think* how my needs were being dismissed, that he didn't care about me and my stress, and that he just did what he wanted for himself. I felt disregarded. I was fuming on the inside and knew this was heading for trouble between us. Realizing my growing anger reaction was more attached to a history of *perceiving* myself as dismissed than this present event, I utilized tonglen. I thought of others who might feel dismissed, rejected or ignored. My thoughts traveled to family, friends and on out into the world accumulating companions in my suffering. Bringing my thoughts back home, aware he too had probably felt the same dismissal, maybe from me, my heart softened. Compassion dispelled my growing wrath. I calmed down thinking, *I can do both the retreat and houseguests. I can do this.* I went to bed and slept peacefully through the night.

The next morning, he brought up what had happened. When I said I thought I could accomplish both the retreat and the house guests, he said he had given it some thought and realized he was thinking of something he wanted and not of me. He intended to call the niece to set another date. Suffering – tonglen – compassion; a spiritual exercise creating a circle of peace.

Spiritual awareness reflects on the absolute depth of human desire. From the day we come into physical existence, we are dependent on other humans who also are in need and are dependent. All persons live in this un-awakened dance of the human and divine dilemma within. In our awareness, we have a will and choices to make on whether we will function from the mind or the heart.

I came to realize how, by identifying with my mind's interpretation and perception of events, I attached my personal value to the work ethic as a reaction to loss. Unconsciously I was attempting to compensate for losing my attachment to my dad when he chose work over me. As the years went by, I innocently attached my self identity to the characteristics of depression. Yet spirituality seeks the truth of relationship, attachment, and desires and disentangles us from what is not true or life-giving to the true self.

The yearning of the self for physical survival is simple yet complex, and the drive of humans to survive is amazing. Yet it was in my awareness of another sense of self, sacred and separate from the human desire for physical ego's striving for self-preservation, that I encountered the healing connection within me. Living primarily in my mind's nature left little awareness of life as a spiritual self. My physical being and self-preservation negated the awareness of my experience of my own soul being. Embedded as I was in my mind, I was almost oblivious of my soul's depth of life in spirit.

My previous understanding of the spiritual life had to do with being good and achieving salvation after this physical existence. However, I have come to realize that the spiritual life is, in fact, the exact opposite. As I came to understand the reality of the pain and misery caused by my mind's attachment to yearnings, desires, and needs in the physical realm, I could willingly release those attachments, opening myself to the possibility of spiritual purpose and meaning.

The best example of this dynamic was my workaholism. It was only when I learned I could actually live and survive without personal value attached to work that I recognized how my false self had been attached to doing. I don't know if I can convey how thoroughly embedded I was in this mental concept of life and living. I was what I *did*. I was what I *thought*. How could I have any value if I was not doing? My parents, teachers, and society unanimously reinforced the agreed-upon mode of living—which was *doing*. I had no concept of myself without doing, so when I *wasn't* doing, my ego had no place to attach its identity and reacted with anxiety and sheer panic.

Eventually I realized that Something was lovingly attentive to me even when I wasn't doing. I had a subtle growing awareness that even if I never did another thing, I was loved. In the stillness of not doing, I sensed love. In the quiet of not thinking, I sensed love. In my darkest time, I was attempting to annihilate my existence that revolved around that which, on another level of living, did not even exist as an issue. Much of the pain had been created by the workings of my mind. When I could still the mind, I was at peace and could feel love as gentle as butterfly wings touching my face—loving, gentle, compassionate, and all-accepting. I only needed to show up in my sacred space in the corner of my home.

Ever so gradually, the panic and anxiety I experienced in my early attempts at meditation and the surges of my ego as it continued to attach itself to doing subsided. I was able to let go of the need to be connected or absorbed by thoughts and doing. I became more and more attracted to and desirous of peace-filled moments that promised the ability to be and exist in another mode of life. The world's way of living seemed less and less desirable, and it was only the spiritual path that seemed to offer satisfaction. I was not satisfied when I was caught up in the world's way of doing life. I was finding an attraction, desire, and satisfaction beyond the mind and the material world, which is so obvious and easily attainable and accessible. Meditation does not come as easily as physical gratifications. However, once one experiences the spiritual benefits of meditation, the way of the world pales and satisfaction with physical gratification wanes, giving over the "work" of meditation to stillness and mindful living. Living mindfully is being aware of what *is* without needing to make it different from *what* it is. One begins to see life from a different perspective.

Sitting quietly is a way to make oneself accessible and available to that which would make itself present, if only it was given the opportunity. Awareness is present during walks in nature, in the beauty of a moment at birth or death, during an indescribable sunset, in the twinkle of the eye at a humorous moment, when a timely comment is made, upon the spontaneous arrival of an unspoken wish—un-captured moments of grace-filled living. I was oblivious to life-giving moments with my depressed mind. Recovery was as if I had awakened after sleepwalking to a more alert physical state of existence; I was aware without judging everything as either good or bad. I realized I had lived unavailable to the life that comes through spiritual awareness. I rarely experienced joy. I rarely accepted what was present before me because generally my mind was either struggling with past events, figuring out what needed to be different, or planning for while fearing the future.

Breath by breath, I could detach from a superficial state of identity and, in so doing, reattach to life on this new level of awareness. What used to satisfy me no longer did, for I was now awake and conscious that it had in fact robbed me of satisfaction—a placebo of living that wasn't working. Something was working in me that I could not access mentally and consciously. It was revealing life to me. All I had to do was stop, observe, and let go of what was so I could become more aware. I was on the threshold of something new that was presenting itself to me.

I had worked through the anxiety of not working and what that meant to me. I had come to accept and appreciate the life space that less activity provided. I found love without doing, and I found my soul when I learned how to be without functioning on the world's standard of living. I realized new awakenings, new desire, and the possibilities of living in a world of life that existed beyond what I had previously perceived quite superficially. I wanted more of this state of being. I desired more and yearned for more. Having escaped my bondage to my mind, I was on the right track—a spiritual path. I left the wilderness that emphasized the mind/world and was liberated to a new land of spiritual practices and soul concepts of peace and love. But to what would I be liberated?

I had experienced the still assurances of love and acceptance. I had written words of wisdom beyond my own thoughts and understanding. Undeniably, something was moving me to experience more moments of a peaceful mind. I suspected I had things yet to learn, and until I knew what was yet unnamed, I had not arrived at my ultimate destination, which I could not fathom. I just knew something more was coming.

Two significant experiences changed my worldview to the point where I could accept my being in this world for the first time. Before these spiritual awakenings, I simply did not want to be in this miserable existence. Life was more difficult than satisfying, more of a struggle than a joy.

The first happened in July 2010. Our church bulletin announced a silent retreat at Mount St. Scholastica Monastery in Atchison, Kansas. As I read about the retreat, I knew my life was backward—I had given more credence to working than to praying. I had life upside down-work over prayer, not prayer before work. With that thought, off I went to my first visit to a monastery and my first experience of a silent retreat. The quiet and stillness of the chapel drew me at different times of the day and night. From the darkness of my soul a thought surfaced that needed expressing, and when it found its way to my consciousness, I voiced it: "God, I'm absolutely not okay with the suffering in this life, and it has everything to do with why I don't want to live on this earth."

The response turned around my thinking and perception about life so totally and completely that it created a desire to live in this world and make a difference where I could. I heard, "Suffering is not the world's. It is mine." Suffering and Christ became one. Although I considered my life miserable, I had, over years of recovery, actually experienced the presence of God as compassion itself in the very roots of grief, loss, suffering, and depression. Pain and suffering are somehow related to Presence.

No human wants to suffer. We are created for survival of the species, to avoid pain and suffering as detrimental to the self. But in the very painful places humankind wants to avoid, God goes where no one else can go, to the center of the created being. God meets us there in our suffering. In suffering, we know and are known by One who shares in the suffering. Suffering is the ultimate place of being known and of being fully, completely loved.

Pain seems to isolate us from one another, because a person believes no one else can really know the extent of his or her suffering. In the silence of suffering only One voice can be heard, the soft whispering presence that says, "I know, I know how you suffer, come to me, only I can give you comfort." The voice of supreme compassion is present in the suffering, and it is only this Presence that can be with a person in the deepest depths of his or her suffering. It was that very voice of Presence that intervened in my times of complete despair. It would take years for me to consciously recognize the whispers as the voice of the Sacred.

It is only this Presence that knows each person's unique spiritual path out of suffering. But in the soul's space, we can feel the connection to what is satisfying and comforting even in pain. We can know the existence and experience of Something More that is moved greatly by compassion in shared suffering.

Western and Eastern spirituality remind us we are in the world but not *of the world*. We are not perfect, but we are loved. We cannot manage life, but there is life being in us. We cannot know the way of life, but we can live the life opened to us. And it is this living presence—the mystery of life lived beneath the obvious—to which we are drawn and that we find satisfying. And what is the satisfying knowledge that complements the awareness of living this life? The truth is that each person is an eternal soul self, conceived in God's love and living within a temporary physical existence. God came to me in my suffering, and so in my suffering I came to know God. I was not alone.

The second occurrence was such a beautiful grace that revealed my deepest truth. As was my custom, I had been sitting by my window, my mind drifting and wondering what I was moving toward in my life. As I looked at the winter scenery outside, a subtle awareness came to my mind that, but for a mere membrane of my physical being, my soul was blended with all creation, visible and invisible, to the expanse of the universe. I then realized that creation—all I could see and beyond—was the thought of God. I realized that I, too, am God's thought manifested, and that all that God is, in God's entirety, is in the thought of me. All that is Supreme is within the thought of me! It was a profound realization of me as the manifested thought of God. Yet there was more to know.

Something deeper than the physical manifestation of my existence was to be found. Something outside caught the corner of my eye—a spark. What is that? It was bright and pulsated like a lightening bug, but that couldn't be, because we were in the dead of winter. Perhaps it was the sun glistening off a leaf? No, because the sun is just coming up and has not come to the west side of the house. Everything is in the shadow of the house. Then I had an epiphany! It must be that each of us is a spark of the Spirit of God. As soon as I thought that, the spark disappeared. I knew that my soul was conceived in God's love and manifested to physical existence on this earth. I realized that my true self came from the very being of the Absolute One. I am part and parcel of God who remains hidden and unseen but can be known and experienced. I knew what can only be revealed. Each one of us is of the divine and there is no separation.

I do not believe this awakening could have happened without the grace of my gradual understanding and compassionate ability within my own being to accept myself. Soulfully knowing God and knowing I could not be separated from God—that I was part and parcel of God—I was able to decide to meet and accept the truth of myself. Only then was I able to consciously grasp and become fully aware of being human and divine. When we grow in the forgiveness and understanding of human nature and get in touch with the spiritual self, we meet within our self, the human and divine, the body-mind-spirit connection as wholeness.

By choosing openness, honesty, and love, we are freed to know the beauty and magnificence of our own self.

When I reached the exact awareness of the truth of my own being in every cell of my body—the inextinguishable self as one with the divine—the soul not separate but safe from all imperfections and failings—I wondered if this knowing had healed the root of my depression. It felt like a spiritual birth of the truth of my created self. In the months to come this would prove a true intuition, as I have never had another depression episode.

Was my depression really a soul sickness, then? Was it grief over the loss of myself? Was I spiritually sensitive to a sense of separation from God after my physical birth? Had I experienced a dark night of the soul, as spoken of in spiritual writings? Yet I was just a child when it began. Was it solely a mental illness? Was depression a soul's dismissal of the value, connectedness, and love of self? Was it a life of separation from God? I don't know if I will find the answer to these questions, but I do know that my search for peace of mind in mental illness was divinely guided through a spiritual healing of the soul, and there I found liberation. I was free. I was delivered from the futile way of living life.

I know who I am. I am that from which I come. I feel I am in the world but not of it, completely. I feel I am within the divine and the divine is within me. When I look into the mirror I see a soul conceived in love. When I look into another's eyes, I know the secret of his or her divine conception. When I view nature, I know I am of the same beauty manifested.

This is the kingdom in which I live now. I no longer live in the bondage of the mind, perceiving, desiring, and enmeshed in that which is only a partial existence,

physical and temporary. The mind does its thing and I
am aware of it, but I do not attach to its functions and
antics. The mind is about what it is created to do. The
mind's ego demands attention. "Look at me, look at me."
It wants to act out for attention like a two-year-old child.
I let it function and remind it of its spiritual origin. It
doesn't have to have everything it used to demand. I
remind myself of my deepest yearnings and desire—that
which I have found within myself.

I return to the scene from the movie *A Beautiful Mind*
in which John Nash, who has schizophrenia, uses his
intellect and will *not* give attention to the personalities
he sees and hears because he knows they are not real. I
consider my mind in the same way. Let it be, but attach
instead to the reality, existence, and function of my soul
being. This kingdom of love, presence, and compassion is
the human existence in this temporary world, but eternal
in that these do not fade. The purposeful unfolding for
my own manifestation is the spiritual way of my day-
to-day living in seeking my God. To discover new life is
my desire and joy, as to this breath I remain in existence.
There is more than meets the eye—it is my life attached
to the source of life.

Today I pray, "Lord, I do want to breathe, because
each breath attaches my existence to the reality of your
life breath in me. I want to move with life and have my
being that I might manifest more fully life lived in you,
and in this I am in a state of enthusiastic joy. For this
life I live; thank you." Sitting in stillness, allowing what
is false to reveal itself and eventually flake away, reveals
the true self. Stillness recalls the true state of our spirit

existence within and beyond what is hidden but can be experienced and known. To this only remain open, and seek that which fulfills you. It is within you. The one who seeks Wisdom, finds life (Proverb 8).

LIVING BREATH
AWARENESS

Love expresses the soul. People ask me, "What methods, processes, and spiritual practices did you use in your spiritual path toward peace?" What they are really seeking, however, is the goal, and the manner of attaining the goal is of minimal importance. Whatever your practice, the time given to it is a sacrifice chosen by you, and it will be honored by God's love. God's grace honors you when you choose God. Therefore, know what you seek.

That which you seek can be achieved; it can be yours. I hope these writings inspire you toward a spiritual journey, for it is the hope of the journey that we begin. Choose your journey and know that your choice to journey will have a favorable outcome, for you will experience the desire of your heart. Be faithful. For those who are aware of their spiritual practices, ask, "What is the quality of my decision to practice? Am I committed? Am I ready for another level of practice?"

God is there for the asking. God is there if given a thought, a moment, a desire, a suffering, or a joy. God is there in each flickering thought you give toward the Supreme and in every minute, undetected moment of desire for God. That which you seek you already have! I found it to be so. It overwhelmed my soul to find that God was always where I most needed God to be. I always had what I most desired. I always survived what I could not bear. I always hoped in my hopelessness. God always filled my emptied heart, soul, and mind. Through faithfulness, I loved God in my journey of heart, mind, and soul—and I have been loved.

Love always was, always is, and through eternal measure, always will be. You already are the desire of that which you seek fulfilled within yourself. You just don't know it consciously. It is readying to manifest in its revelation.

Living in love is to live in the suspension between breaths. Trust that the rhythmic inhalation and exhalation is the expression of receiving love and expressing it through giving actions. Love is breath, and living is breathing. Neither love nor living is within human management, other than the annihilation of it—and even then humans have no control over that which is eternal life, even in life's extinguishment. It is to this breath force that life actions are attributed. Go slowly, go gently, be attentive to God, and all that you desire will be brought into being. Do not fear the unknown but trust its attentiveness to God's will.

My daily prayer developed within my heart: "Lord, by all grace, guide me. May my breath still my mind so I can be attentive to loving you. My heart stills in peaceful rest when I am in your Spirit's desire—and in my soul is your loving will for the actions of my mind and hands and feet. May every breath be awareness of your presence, O God, by drawing from your inner chamber, for therein your beloved lives." When my heart and soul are connected, they release the mind's intelligence to know the way of all fruition, serving others with the same love received. Love, then, is the mind, the heart, the body, the soul connection. For me, doing life differently is to do it the way of breath, love, intuition of heart, and inspiration of soul, for therein life resides. Life is from the heart, from the center, a particle of the Universe's expression.

Every thought you have that consciously connects with God connects with God's consciousness of you, and from God's thought is your existence. God consciousness opens, expands, releases, and flows with life force from your trickling stream to the expanse of the Universe's magnanimous life force. You are connected to this magnanimous life force. Trust it, believe it, live it, feel it, know it. Awareness is the portion expanding the understanding of the Universe as one, and all possibilities are yours for the loving expression of the effort and will to live the desires of God.

LIVING FOR GOD

When I realized my origin in the Creator, when I knew my true identity, my depression was gone. I was free, liberated from a mental illness I had lived with all my life. My mind, body, and spirit/soul are at peace, all working in harmonious cooperation in the same life goal—to live from the soul. In essence, through divine grace, my relationship to myself and the world around me entered a new way of being one.

I am no longer at odds within myself because my spirituality—the relationship between the Supreme, the self, and other—are as one. There was one more liberation to come to make my peace complete, however. I found it within the stillness of my mind, where it lurked in the shadows. My mind is quiet now; until it became silent, I hadn't noticed the noise it made. The stillness became more complete after my final anxiety was resolved, uprooted by grace.

Early events in my childhood seemed to have created memory cords of particularly tenacious fears that settled, hidden, in a low-grade, almost imperceptible anxiety within me. Perhaps these cables of thoughts exist to hold our damaged egos together, which enables our defenses to maintain vice-like holds on us. It is when we gradually let go of our attempts to control life, manage the self, and gratify the senses that we discover the existence of the binding cords of our thoughts. It seems much of what I was seeking in life's pleasure were attempts to soothe or avoid the residue of uncomfortable memories.

Even to consider loosening these familiar cords can create fear, anxiety, or even panic, as when I stopped working. Such feelings and reactions are dependable indicators of the existence of these cords of thoughts and feelings. Although one may be able to discover the cords and even determine their roots with fair accuracy, it is only grace that can dislodge, disconnect, and sever their deepest hold in the psyche. Until they are severed, they will have a hold on us. Until my cords were released, I was not aware of their pervasive binding entanglement. Until I was freed, I did not realize their effect on my well-being.

Ironically, I was at a spiritual workshop on my perpetual quest to learn more when my cords were released. I was given an opportunity through prayer to offer something to God that seemed blocked in me. In my mind's eye, I saw a stream. The flow of the water was hampered by a pile of debris and sticks, like a beaver's dam. The water flowed, though it was significantly impaired. I named this pile of debris "fear" and asked God to disentangle it and free the fear so the water could flow freely. Although I did not consciously make the image change, suddenly the pile of sticks was gone from my mind's eye. In its place a simple white chrysanthemum floated beautifully, freely, and unimpeded on crystal clear water. Other than realizing I could not re-image the dam, I didn't know what to make of the prayer exercise, but I knew something had happened.

Later in the day, someone asked me how preparations were going for a workshop I was facilitating. I explained that, while I had not planned it, a few alterations had just come about seemingly of their own accord, so I was accepting these changes as part of what needed to happen.

"Well," she said, "you don't really have to know for things to happen." These words struck me like words of gold; they seemed so clear and true. I went downstairs for coffee and someone else asked how the day was going. I told her what had just happened and she said with a smile that as she got older she realized she really does not need to know because the Spirit seems to works things out. She added, "You really *never* needed to know."

By the time I returned upstairs, I felt like a lifetime of pain and anxiety had just been cleansed from my soul/ spirit. I wanted to cry for the relief of it. In grade school I had suffered so much because of my inability to make A's and B's, the only grades that were satisfactory. It created years of anxious misery for me. I thought if I was smarter I would not be so miserable and suffer so much from not knowing what I needed to know or should know. As my life progressed, when it came to education, I just kept going, achieving degrees and certificates in an attempt to know enough. I attended every workshop I could to try to fulfill my desire for enough knowledge.

I thought if I only knew enough and was smart enough, all would go well. I know now that *if only* is a phrase used by those who grieve. *If only* comments indirectly address the underlying pain and are an attempt to take the pain away. *If only* expresses a wish or searches for a way to have prevented pain in the past or to prevent it in the future. As a child I thought that *if only* I was different, this pain wouldn't be happening. I spent my life and a great deal of money to feed this voracious idea. And in an afternoon, after a simple prayer, it was gone. Truth suddenly broke through years of thinking and my obsession that I did not know enough. The sword of truth cut the cord that bound my spirit to fear. *What* we know cannot hold a candle to *knowing* the One who can't be known, but who reveals even to the foolish. *Soul* smart is all the value above brain smart. And my futile addiction to getting smart enough turned to ashes.

I could not have told you consciously that this gnawing anxiety existed until I was free of it and was finally at peace. The idea was done, gone, expended, dissipated into the ethereal space of light and healing. *I don't have to know everything. I never had to know.* How liberating! My mind is now free from the insatiable, hungry tiger of the intellect. I am appeased in what is worth knowing. My underlying anxiety, like an undetected electrical hum in my soul, was quieted. Both my mind and soul are now at peace.

So much was hidden in my mind and soul. I don't believe any human could reveal its silent workings. Who could have known—or, if the existence of unconscious thoughts and feelings had been brought to consciousness, who could have extricated them from my mind and soul? Who could know the tenacious and destructible thoughts, beliefs, and false values that inhibited me from freely living in happiness, love, truth, and joy? It seems such an undertaking is in the realm of God, who has total and complete knowledge, Pure Awareness, of all that is within us. It is God's truth that liberates us, cutting through and severing what is not truth within us. This experience does not minimize the value I found in psychotherapy support, but it was the inter-relatedness, the love experience of God within my soul, that healed my deepest, darkest depth of depression. How could I, or any human, have ferreted out untruths from the dark recesses of the mind and escorted them to the light? Could any human cauterize the wound with healing truth to such a degree that it would not return again?

I am in awe of how God's love and care continue to act with the purpose of liberating me more fully that I might know life more and more. The journey I have traveled thus far fosters only joy and trust that what God has begun will continue until my last breath here on earth.

I don't know if I am anywhere close to adequately loving God enough for all the grace and healing, hope and joy, and liberation and life I have received. All I can attempt to do is to give God the only thing I have to give—my life and all that I am. I know I only have me to offer in my surrender and attaching to God. I was graced with knowing who I am, so the giving of myself and my life feels like a zero call, because all I am and all I have is gift. I believe God receives this response as gratitude and so honors every little bitty thing I offer as willingness to receive all God would give. Through surrendering my life, I can love and serve the Supreme One's purpose for my created life. In receiving all God would give, I in turn give God glory for my own giftedness and live out my unique purpose while here on earth. When this life is done, I have a deep sense I will return to the womb of God from which I came.

All I have told you has come about on the basis of the deal God and I made years ago; some persons would call it a covenant, I suppose. In this covenant I agreed I would surrender my miserable life existence with depression to a Higher Power's care, and in exchange that Higher Power would manage my unmanageable depression. So far, it has worked out pretty great. I am spiritually aware enough to realize absolutely from where life, my life, comes. With every breath I am loved, healed, and grateful.

Perhaps in the reading of this book you and I have been one in our suffering. May we also be one in our joy as we share in the One who makes life whole, as God's kingdom comes to us while we are yet here on earth. We do not need to leave this world to find the peace we seek. It is within us now. We are connected to it. It is as Breath itself. You are sustained by breath. You are breathed into this life—in stillness, breathe with it consciously, and know love. Conscious of breath, you will know life.

BREATHING AS
A CONSCIOUSNESS
OF GOD

Are you breathing? If your answer is "Yes," it is a very reliable indication that you are alive. In our concern for others at critical times, we ask, "Is he/she breathing?" Breath is a sign that the person is still with us and is not separated from us, whereas not breathing is a sign of death.

Out of concern for our spiritual rather than our physical well-being, we would do well to ask, "Am I conscious of my breath? To what is my breath attached?" Although generally we are not *physically* unconscious, in our busyness and absorption with life on the level of human nature, we often are *spiritually* unconscious. One way to be spiritually conscious—that is, to be connected with life on the mystical level of gift, grace, and love—is to be conscious of our breath and to whom it is attached.

Whether we practice breath awareness during quiet meditation or in each day-to-day experience through mindfulness, this conscious connectedness to breath brings new life awareness to enhance our existence and the quality of living. It is amazing and wondrous that our breath rhythms and patterns change in direct response to physical situations; for example, the breath quickens and readies us when we are fearful, indicates our rising body stress, and eases the mind with simple focus on its presence.

Attentiveness to breath and its source can significantly enhance the quality of moments and events in our life. To know the source of our breath is to create the body-mind-spirit connection that can affect tranquility and stability at any time. Breath awareness is always available to us in any circumstance.

Just recently two stories in my local newspaper illustrated how breath consciousness saved lives. The people in both stories attributed their survival of life-threatening vehicle accidents to their practice of meditation. In the seconds before the crashes occurred, they connected to their breath, relaxed, and took the appropriate actions, thus avoiding fatal injuries. In one incident, a woman had the presence of mind to lie down on the seat when a semi-trailer pulled out in front of her. The top of her car was sheared off, but her injuries were minor. In another story, a woman crushed by an overturned all-terrain vehicle was suffocating as she waited for help to arrive. Resorting to her meditation practice, she relaxed and was able to make her breath shallow enough to survive until she was rescued.

Depression and anxiety felt as dramatic for me as these examples of physical survival. Even a small event or thought could trigger a drop into depression. However, I learned that by being as aware as one is in the face of an oncoming accident, I could decide to be conscious of my breath when I detected a sign of distress in my body. By focusing on the breath, I was able to ease through the potential crisis and avoid a decline into depression.

I could feel in my body the physical sensation of "dropping" and use it as my first clue that something I was thinking was causing me distress.

I named the technique I used my ABC's: *A*ware, *B*reathe, *C*onsciousness. I would attend to the thought, if I could catch it, breathing with it. Thoughts create feelings, so I would breathe with that feeling by trying to name it. I learned to be inquisitive; I would ask, "What is the name of this feeling, and what does if feel like?" The sooner I could stop and think "Just breathe, Sharon, just breathe," the better off I would be in riding it through and the more I could avoid tripping into the downward slide. If need be, my mantra would extend for a while— "I am breathing the breath of God; all is well"—until the emotion passed. Instead of assuming thoughts and feelings as myself, I developed the ability to detach from them while giving them some attention, then moved on to treat myself with compassion, *not* recrimination for believing them or for feeling anxiety or fear.

I believe that the A.B.C. steps in breath awareness track well with the first three steps of a twelve-step program. To review: Step one is awareness of the unmanageable. Step two is an awareness of the inability to sanely respond to circumstances based solely on myself. I needed help. Step three is turning over the situation and one's life willingly to the care of a Higher Power. Breath awareness, in short, is a pause tool for making the moment-to-moment decision to attach to God as one's life source instead of attaching to the thought, feeling, event, or temptation to feed one's hungry tiger of desire or reaction. Breath awareness provides the means of transcending and transforming the happening event and its potential consequences.

By attaching to breath in critical moments of depression or anxiety, I was able to prevent my thoughts and emotions from triggering a depression plummet. One who practices breath meditation and breath awareness can become poised and balanced in each moment where they might previously have reacted. The balance and stability represent the conscious connection to Something Greater than the event. "What about crisis, trauma, and feelings?" you might ask. Breath awareness is like the Tommy Tippy Cup of the 1950s. The weight of the sand in the bottom of the cup prevents it from tipping over. Breath awareness is my Tommy Tippy Cup.

Having been *un*connected to my breath and its source for many years, *being* connected to my breath is now a critical part of my self-awareness. Breath is the soul life realization of where I come from and where I have my being, and that realization keeps me connected to breath. God transformed and transcended my aversion relationship to breathing. The life breath we connect with and initiate in meditation can be connected with again and again expanding meditation's calming breath throughout the day, if need be.

The awareness of one's breath and existence as the breath of God gives the soul experiences of joy. In relaxing breath, God breath, sighing releases anxiety and tenseness, reminding you that Presence is available to you. In particularly stressful times, as you breathe, imagine that your breath is connected to the universe's breath rhythms, empowering all possibilities of care and resource. Remind yourself that all created beauty exchanges oxygen, and as you connect with breath, you are one with all beauty beyond your unpleasant thoughts and feelings.

I once experienced this sensation vividly and am able to draw on it from memory. I had driven from Kansas to Colorado in silence with the radio turned off, just bringing my thoughts back to breath when they wandered. As I turned north off I-70, I was overwhelmed with the beauty and spaciousness of the sky and land, and at the same time I felt just as expanded. I remember my joy as I thought, "I could do anything I set myself to, because life is full of possibilities!" A sign of God's work in healing is the awareness of new ways of thinking different than the depression's habitual thinking patterns of "I can't" and "I'm not enough."

I encourage you to engage in the simple practice of breath awareness, for in breath's conscious connection to God, all potential is assured and all is well. If you are breathing, all is well, for you are connected with God. If you are not breathing, you also will know that all is well, for you are with God. Breathe. Be conscious of the source of your breath and you will be consciously connected to God. In your breath, life is hidden, and all its potential waits for you. Surrender. Say yes.

Does breath awareness work 100% of the time in preventing feelings or reactions? No. There are life events that can trigger something from my history and I can feel overwhelmed, out of balance, angry, confused or frustrated. What is different is that I don't fall into a depression. What is different is that I can tolerate feelings. I try to stay mindful of what is happening. I return to stillness, to listening from within, asking for understanding, enlightenment and healing. I call a friend and talk about what's normal in my sadness or anger because with depression every feeling seemed extreme. And I wait. It might take a bit of time for understanding to come to light, but when it does it is usually awakens me more to myself, to the human dilemma and to spiritual truth. I no longer fall with these events. I resurrect.

EPILOGUE

It is a windy spring day as I write. The wind is toying with the freshly planted spring flowers, but they are well rooted, well grounded in their fresh dirt. They are unconcerned with the wind's antics.

The tulips are dancing as they are buffeted about. They consider themselves waving to passersby who admire their beauty. They do not fear the wind because they, too, are grounded well in their bulbs, weighted with earth, roots grasping the earth below.

We are no less rooted in Spirit. On the surface of the earth, be it of nature or of human workings, events can play havoc with us, battering us about in efforts to win us over or yank us free of our moorings. My story indicates the fragility of my moorings when I am not aware, alert, and attentive to my own grounding. When I was not aware, I was nearly uprooted in my fragile and vulnerable mental, emotional, and spiritual health.

Nature teaches us of the earth's tenacious hold on what grounds life through drastic events, such as in the aftermath of a volcano. Eventually some little sprig of life pops its head from the ashes, and mountains become green again. Nature teaches us that we need to be mindful of our grounding in the same spirit of life. On the continuum from simple to drastic, we learn what is vividly true of this life force if we are attentive and aware.

Your ground is your center. Your center is your life root. Within the Spirit, weavings permeate the whole above you, below you, to your right and to your left, in front of you and behind you. If we are only aware of the exterior aspects of our life, we are not grounded, and life can tear at us and threaten to uproot us. If we remain conscious of the interior aspects of our life and are aware that our being is grounded in the life Source, although the winds may blow and buffet us, we are at peace.

We fear when we do not know that which grounds us. Know who made the winds. Then, regardless of the winds that blow, you will remain assured with courage, strength, hope, and faith in all that remains unseen but is vital and available to you. Let nothing disturb your peace as you remain conscious that no matter what happens, there is more, so much more hidden in it. Look there, into the mystery of it, and find a piece of life, peace in life, that you would not have found but for the mind and heart and all your might's experience of it. Be tenaciously grounded into the unknown. It is everything you desire and it is that Desire that absorbs you, body, mind, and spirit—if you will it.

> Live –know your breath and be conscious of its Source connection.
>
> In this way, you live connected to the cause of all life –your life.
>
> Breathe it out and breathe it in.
>
> Breathe life into Being.
>
> Breathe it into being.

There are no life concerns, if one remains in breath, for the breath of God is above all else to be named Jesus-the name above all that one could name, so leave off naming anything other than naming it in Christ who is above all and without Him nothing comes into being.

Let the Lord name for you what is, for His word is above what you would name something and your name falls short of what really is.

Seek the Lord for anything to be named.

Seek not your own understanding, for your understanding falls short of the true name for what God brings into existence.

Let the name of Jesus be the name for what you do not understand and leave the life occurrence there, in the name of Christ, to be named by Christ.

AFTERWORD

A few months have passed since I've written the final book chapter. In this opportunity before publishing, I want to share something that completes the journey from where my story began. You have faithfully traveled with my soul's struggle from inadequate childhood attachments to finding a relationship with the Divine through stillness. More has come, and I want to share its beauty with you.

I was struggling with a relationship. We couldn't put our finger on the problem, but it was disturbing in its awkward tension. My spiritual director suggested I "sit with it in stillness, mindfulness and awareness." While it took a few weeks of not thinking about the relationship, but just being with it, the waiting bore insight and healing to my poverties that began in non-attachment to my mother and father.

The first to surface was an awareness of what I would describe as a chronic irritability. When sitting with the irritability, I found an underlying, almost primitive fear and overcompensating behaviors as defensive measures. Sitting in silence, vulnerable as an infant, slowly a great sense of a benevolent presence seemed to bless the world around me with nurturing and giving that I could find trustworthy. I named her Mother Benevolence.

A few days later, in stillness, I knew the battle is not with others, but with the power of the dark shadows of the mind. As a child of God, I was asked to see, not with my own eyes, but to see with a spiritual way of seeing as the Father sees-without judgment of my own perceptions. One of the great illusions of earth is that one looks at others, or reacts to others, as if they are darkness. I wonder if this is the greatest of deceptions. Equanimity and love are to see all through the Father's eyes. To put on the mind of Christ is to see as the Father sees. First, I was to strive with effort to see myself as the Father's child. Second, I was to pause, to see all else as the Father sees what is before me.

My friends, I then fully realized what it meant in the hospital to hear, "You will be delivered." 1 Peter reminded me I was delivered from the futile way of life your fathers handed on to you, not by any diminishable sum of silver or gold, but by Christ's blood. Our faith and hope are centered in God. My heart was transferred from earthly to spiritual adoption. I felt the meaning of being adopted as a child of God. To do life differently was to live this spiritual way of life.

My earliest sufferings and poverty, inadequate attachment to my earthly parents, could not begin to meet my deepest spiritual needs which I have found in Benevolence and a sense that I am truly a child of God. God's love satisfies our poverties. I am home, my friend, truly home. Do not fear darkness, but go there to find the Light waiting for you. You are already home. Become aware of it. Colossians 1 says we are filled with the knowledge of God's will through perfect wisdom and spiritual insight. We are rescued from the power of darkness and brought into the kingdom. Be still and know who God is in you.

Questions for Reflection and Group Study

Chapter 1:

Where Does Grace Begin?

- Are you aware of times in your life when you were prompted to do something different or to change course? If so, what type of struggle did those situations entail?

- What was the outcome of making or not making a decision to do something different?

- Do you believe this process was the spirit of God working in your life?

- Have you ever had an unexpected experience of the presence of God? If so, what were the circumstances of your life at the time? Would you consider that period as a time of spiritual transition?

- How does it feel to consider the possibility that the very presence of God has been lovingly intervening in and guiding your life?

CHAPTER 2: MEDITATION AND SPIRITUAL PRACTICES

- Can you think of any times you felt the desire or prompting to be quiet and still?

- Do you find yourself gravitating toward being in a place of solitude? For example, do you desire to take walks in nature, feel urges to get away, and seek the space and the opportunity to be alone in your home?

- Do you ever find yourself listing reasons why you can't be still and quiet?

- When you feel the desire to be still, do you think God could be calling you to be quiet in response to your own prayers for assistance?

- Can you respond to the prompting to be silent by creating a sacred space and dedicating 15 minutes a day to be faithful to the desire working in you?

- Have you ever kept a journal? Would it be helpful to reflect on your experience with silence by keeping a journal entitled, "My Spiritual Journey of Stillness"?

Sharon Highberger   113

CHAPTER 3:
LIVING IN GRACE

- Are you currently going through a difficult period in your life, or have you experienced such a time in the past?

- Are you aware of a sense of desire or yearnings within your heart, even though they are unnamed?

- Do you have a sense that "there must be something more than this"?

- What thoughts keep you from acting on your urges and promptings to do something different?

- As you become more consciously aware of your inner promptings, can you attend to them with a renewed, hope-filled, "Yes"?

- Can you acknowledge the possibility that underlying the difficulties you are encountering, grace may be present and working in a positive and transformative way for your own good?

- Can you lay down any fears and anxieties about your present circumstances, trusting that a benevolent Spirit will receive what you surrender?

- Can you believe that an infinite compassionate presence has taken you and your life into its care?

CHAPTER 4: THE ULTIMATE SURRENDER

- Have you had a circumstance or period in your life that was particularly painful or difficult?

- What options did you consider to get away from the pain and difficulties?

- Do you remember surrendering to the pain or to God?

- What thoughts, events, or interventions influenced or changed your course?

- What difference might it make to hope or believe that divine intervention was available to you?

- Is it possible that the events were significant movements in your spiritual journey to God?

- What does it mean to say that in the death of what is happening, new life will come?

CHAPTER 5: DIVORCING THE MIND

- Have you ever found yourself seeking and searching in ways that were different from your usual methods of discovery? If so, what did you learn from your new approach?

- Do you identify yourself as your mind?

- What does it mean to you to hear you are not your mind?

- How does hearing that you are not your mind support or validate new senses of intuition within you?

- Do you ever find yourself believing or questioning the workings of your mind?

- Are you conscious of your mind as being separate from your true self as it is found in your soul?

CHAPTER 6: LIBERATING THE SOUL

- Can you draw from memory an experience where you felt unconditionally loved?

- Do you return to the truth of that experience in such a way as to only allow yourself loving thoughts toward yourself?

- Are you really aware of a presence within your own soul?

- From where do you draw your source of living? Can you make a firm decision regarding what you will listen to—your mind or your heart/soul?

CHAPTER 7: LIVING IN THE KINGDOM OF THE SOUL

- Do you question that there is more to life than you consciously know?

- Do you yearn for more but cannot name the desire?

- Can you surrender and say yes to what you cannot name?

- What life experience tells you that your life is unfolding and revealing?

- Can you look at areas of your life and see them in stages of bondage-wilderness-liberation or kingdom?

- Do you find within yourself disharmonies between your body, mind, and spirit/soul connections?

- Name what is most unmanageable to you and lay it lovingly at the feet of God. How does that feel to you?

CHAPTER 8: LIVING BREATH AWARENESS

- What are your spiritual practices? (For example, prayer, meditation, spiritual reading, religious ritual, yoga, nature walks, or art.)

- How faithful are you in your practices?

- Can you renew your commitment to journey with the Supreme?

- What life "aha" moments go beyond thoughts and words for you? (Examples may include sunsets, laughter, and beauty.)

- Can you believe in life's mystery and love more deeply than your known self and world experience?

CHAPTER 9: LIVING FOR GOD

- What spiritual experiences have moved you forward in understanding your value?

- What spiritual experiences have enlightened you as to who you are to God?

- What differences have these enhancements meant to you and the quality of your life?

- How have spiritual experiences made a difference in loving God and/or loving others?

- What life events can you point to that mark a shift from the way you were before they happened to the way you were after their occurrence?

- What fear or anxiety would you like to give over to God's healing compassion?

CHAPTER 10: BREATHING AS A CONSCIOUSNESS OF GOD

Breathing Practices:

- Pay attention to your breath as you go about your daily activities. What effect does this practice have on you?

- Be aware that each breath is your connectedness to God as breath. How does this awareness affect you?

- When you experience anger, fear, or panic, pay attention to your breath instead of the thought. Does this practice contribute to your well-being?

- In trying circumstances, instead of getting upset or involved, take a break and sit quietly, focusing only on your breath. You may need to return to this practice a number of times to remain calm and detached. Does this practice help you cope with life's difficulties?

- When all is well and you are aware of where your breath comes from, what feelings arise?

BIBLIOGRAPHY

Pema Chödrön, When Things Fall Apart. Boston: Shambhala, 2005

Eckhart Tolle, The Power of Now. Vancouver, B.C., Canada. Namaste, 1999

Mark Williams, John Teasdale, Zindel Segal, and Jon Kabat-Zinn, The Mindful Way through Depression" Freeing Yourself From Chronic Unhappiness. New York: Guilford, 2007